CCNA:
Quick Reference
Guide to CCNA
Terminology
&
Concepts

Walter Joseph Schenck, Jr.

A+, ENP, CCNA, MCP, MCSE

Enterprise Networking Professional Certification
Florida State University, 1999

A+ & CCNA
Florida Community College at Jacksonville, 2000

CCNA: Quick Reference Guide to CCNA
Terminology & Concepts

ISBN-13: 978-1548231231
ISBN-10: 1548231231

Printed in the United States of America

Warning and Disclaimer

This study guide is designed to provide information about CCNA. I have made every effort to make sure this book is as complete and as accurate as possible, but no warranty or fitness is implied.

The information is provided on an "as is" basis. The author, nor any party, nor Cisco Systems, Inc., shall have neither liability nor responsibility to any person or entity with respect to any loss or damage arising from the information contained in this book or from the use of this material.

The contents expressed in this book belong to the author and are not necessarily those of Cisco Systems, Inc.

Legal Notice

This material is not sponsored, endorsed or affiliated with Cisco Systems, Inc. Cisco, Cisco Systems, by any other program that is aligned with CCNA.

Dedication

To my wife who lost many hours of sleep trying to keep up with all the things that interest me.

One day soon, the time will come when our hands will embrace and hold gently throughout the afternoon.

Table of Contents

Foreword

This quick reference guide is intended to get to the heart and meat of Cisco terminology and the values associated with them. I don't believe CCNA books should be cluttered with additional material, other than facts, facts, and more facts.

Because there are no short-cuts to mastering the CCNA material, I deliberately repeated key points to reinforce what is being taught.

This book should be read several times. It is also geared toward taking the CCNA exam. You may fail the exam the first time you take it, but don't worry if you do. Many who work in the field cannot pass the test. Friends and relatives originally got them their jobs. If you fail the test, do not give up on taking it again and again, if necessary. It'll feel like a money crunching waste of time, but today's employers require the certification. Friends and relatives can only go so far. If nothing else, having taking the test, you'll have experienced the methodology that Cisco uses against the test-taker. Believe me, it is not their goal to see you pass. Cisco makes life miserable in the testing room.

I am not going to be asking questions in this book, because I do not believe that by reading a question and having me provide you with the answer will be strong enough to spark the electrical charges in your brain to recall the material during testing time. To pass the test will require for you to conduct a peculiar analysis of the question. By being fully armed with the facts, it may get you home. The sun always rises in the east, and no matter how weird the question, there is(are) correct, discernible answer(s). It is important that you read the question twice or even three times. Lastly, there are many sites out there that will provide you with excellent pre-testing material.

But, I also have to tell you, there can be no guarantees that you will pass the CCNA exam just because you read this book. I cannot control your study habits or inspire you to achieve and strive toward something that may not be in your cards to conquer. It is going to take a lot of hard reading, concentration, memorization, repeat reading, and forcing your mind to face the perils of a strange encounter. Ultimately, there is just you and the lonely night. Distress will come. Grab a cup of coffee, or soda pop, and vanquish the fear of the night to come to terms with what you are about to encounter: the CCNA test.

And, actually, that is why I wrote this book. I wrote this book to act as a highly focused guide for you to quickly refer to the facts surrounding CCNA questions.

I will be using bold text here and there to force your eyes to alert your mind that there is an important fact being presented to you. I am also italicizing to permit your eye to distinguish an important fact from another fact.

There are many box and table presentations in this book. The reason I created them around the text is to tell the eye to enforce a mental image on the material being presented.

I use as many enhancers as I can to make the eye and the mind work together. On occasion I try a lit odd humor to make you smile and wonder: what kind of guy is this?

Anyway, please strive to succeed in your endeavor of reading this material. The time frame to learn this material is about three months. If you are an advance student, with prior exposure, you can easily use this guide as a two to three day cram reading. It will definitely reacquaint you with forgotten or dismissed terms and the way of visualizing things for the test.

Should a beginner read this book? Well, I wrote it for you. I love the beginner who defeats the world and achieves grand success. I do not believe in the mote expression, "Today is the first day of the rest of your life" because every morning presents a brand new belief and happenstance. But, yes, I do believe that we must "Seize the Day" and make what we can of it. One day follows another. One word leads to a sentence and that sentence leads to a paragraph. The heart's expression is to conquer and triumph what others may fail at. What shines more brightly: a man's spirit or the stars?

Thus, you must not fail. Study hard. Turn off the TV for a little while. Then, realistically, take a deserved break. Turn on the TV for an hour, and then get back to studying again.

Three things should guide you: achievement, pride, and stature. When you pass the CCNA test, you will, in that specific demonstration of you ability, conquer the world. The dizzying heights that plagued you, will pale to insignificance because you had strived and struggled and defeated the demons that held you back.

You may not get a job, but boy, that certification is a wonder to behold! Ten thousand others failed to achieve it, but you overcame and demanded an excellence of performance that the ordinary person will never attain or comprehend.

By the way, it was this guide that finally got me through the CCNA exam!

You are great!

The OSI Layers

Open Systems Interconnect Layer		
Number	**Protocol**	**Function**
7	Application	synchronizes communication, resource allocation
6	Presentation	encryption, **translation**, and compression
5	Session	**dialogue management**, service requests and responses
4	Transport	UDP, TCP, paths, **data segments**
3	Network	**routers**, logical addressing, multiple data links, **IP**, IPX, **ICMP**
2	Data Link	**Switches**, Bridges, **physical addressing**, network topology
	MAC Sublayer	*Multiple devices, protocol access*
	LLC Sublayer	*manages communications to upper-level protocols, **SNAP**, independent status,*
1	Physical	**hubs**, repeaters, amplifiers, electrical, Ethernet, synchronized bits, data rates

The Upper layers are known as the Application, Presentation, and Session Layer. Collectively, these three comprise the **Application Layer** of the OSI Model

Whereas, the lower layers: the Transport, the Network, the Data-Link and the Physical Layers are collectively referred to as the **Data Transport** area.

The OSI (Open Systems Interconnect) model can be defined as a **layered model** that is used by vendors and engineers to help them integrate new changes without affecting the other layers because the networking functions are separated into **discrete subset** layers.

The OSI model is a conceptual framework. It is not a specific application that demands exact protocol usage.

keywords

- multivendor integration

- Isolates changes to a single layer

- Creates and implements network standards for devices and for internetworking plans

- Modular fashion

- Discrete subset layers

- Interoperable technology that utilizes standardized interfaces which help to reduce complexity and **simplify** the learning process.

When a person wants to learn something new, first they must acquaint themselves with the terminology. Next, learn the foundation that is being presented to you. After this, try to grasp the expansive picture rather than the miniaturization of things. Did not Theus conquer the man-bull? Reduce the complex to its simple terms.

That's what's happening here. A vendor can work his newly developed applications within the frame of what exists without worrying about having to invent new protocols as the layers are already separated into manageable subsets.

Because each layer works as a peer-to-peer communication system, they contain within their framework a series of packets referred to Protocol Data Unit (**PDU**). The PDUs contain control information in their headers and trailers. In the upper three layers, the PDU's point directly to their corresponding layer in the other system. The upper layer protocols also rely on the **SDU** (Service Data Unit) which also provides headers inside their frames to lead the packets to their proper destination.

ANSI (American National Standards Institute and ISO (International Standards Organization) helped to develop the OSI model in 1974 in Geneva, Switzerland.

NOTE

The hierarchical model works on
the Access layer level, the Distribution layer level,
and the Core layer level

Application Error
Level 7

- The Application Layer **synchronizes** the sending and receiving applications: synchronizes communication.

- The Application Layer can work with E-mail through any Internet Browser. The Application Layer can work with any spreadsheet program, with Photoshop, has file transferring abilities, and the Application Layer permits two opposing sides fight it out over the Internet with Video games.

- The Application Layer intensifies the availability of the intended communication partner. It **identifies the user interface** that forms the communication partnership.

- The Application Layer determines if **sufficient and appropriate resources** are present to establish a connection for the intended destination node.

- The Application Layer determines resource availability and makes sure that communication exists.

- The Application Layer verifies the identity of the destination computer and that the appropriate resources are present to establish a connection.

NOTE

The Application Layer uses **Telnet** to verify the application program's connectivity

Application Layer Protocols	
Telnet	Terminal Emulation
FTP	File Transfer Protocol *(multichanneled)*
FTAM	File Transfer Access and Management
SMTP	Simple Mail Transport Protocol *(UDP & IP)*
VTP	Virtual Terminal Protocol
CMIP	Common Management Information Protocol
WWW	World Wide Web
EDI	Electronic Data Interchange
WAIS	Wide Area Information Server
SNMP	Simple Network Mail Protocol
DNS	Domain Name Server
HTTP	Hyper Text Transport Protocol

CMIP and SNMP provide management utilization information

CMIP is a function of DECnet

SNMP relies on MIB (Management Information Base) to create a report on the network as it is being monitored

Presentation Layer

Level 6

- The Presentation Layer is used to **translate** text and data syntax between applications. It also performs **file conversions**.

- The Presentation layer represents the translating function of the OSI Model.

- The Presentation Layer **negotiates** the **data transfer syntax** between ASCII and EBCDIC.

To translate EBCDIC to ASCII the Presentation Layer uses Abstract Syntax Notation

- The Presentation Layer **performs data compression** services and data **encryption** services.

This translation process helps to maintain system independent process for the vendors

- The Presentation Layer **provides services to the end users** and helps them manage the session between hosts

To perform this, the Presentation layer will negotiate the data through a representation process

- The Presentation Layer can also work with the services of a **Redirector**

Translation Services from Vendor to User		
ASCII	JPEG	MPEG
EBCDIC	GIF	Quick Time
	TIFF	MIDI
	PICT	

MPEG stands for Motion Pictures Experts Group

JPEG stands for Joint Photographic Experts Group

TIFF stands for Tagged Image File Format

MIDI stands for Musical Instrument Digital Interface

Keywords

compression, JPEG, ASCII, data representation

Session Layer

Level 5

Protocols	
RPC	Remote Procedure Call
ZIP	Zone Information Protocol
SCP	Session Control Protocol
NFS	Network File System
ASP	AppleTalk Session Protocol
SQL	Structured Query Language
X Window	Unix terminal usage
DNA SCP	Digital Network Architecture Session Control Protocol
NetBIOS	Windows 98, and NT usage

NFS is used by SUN Microsystems and Unix. NFS functions through TCP/IP

DNA SCP is used by DECnet Phase IV. It is used to establish and terminate logical link services

ZIP functions under AppleTalk. ZIP is used to maintain a network number-to-zone name mappings in the AppleTalk routers.

ASP establishes and maintains sessions between an Apple server and its client

NOTE

A portion of the SMTP can utilize the Session Layer whenever it uses the UDP and IP protocols for message exchanges

- The Session Layer consists of service requests and service responses among different network devices *(nodes)*

- The Session Layer coordinates the dialog between two communicating application processes

- The Session Layer keeps the sending and receiving station from sending segments at the same time: Dialogue management

Provides dialogue management between devices that run applications

- The Session Layer establishes, creates, manages, maintains and terminates (ends) sessions between applications.

- The Session Layer **coordinates** communications between systems through a **synchronization process** by utilizing **checkpoints**, terminations, and restarts between the applications.

An Overview of Switch Utilization

A Short overview is provided to help you understand the relationship between the Session Layer and the Switches

The Session Layer is the key area through which the Full Duplex, Half Duplex and Simplex switches work through to establish, restart, and terminate dialogue between the applications

3 modes of communication	
Simplex	One device transmits while another listens
Half-duplex	It either transmits or it listens. It uses one pair of wires
Full-duplex	It transmits and receives at the same time. It uses two pairs of wires

---

Full duplex Ethernet doubles throughput

There are no collisions of frames in full duplex Ethernet as it does not rely on CSMA/CD

To implement Full Duplex Ethernet:

First, all network cards *(NICs)* must support
full duplex Ethernet,
as should all the other connectivity devices

Second, you must disable the loopback and collision
detection methods in the switch

Transport Layer

Level 4

- The Transport Layer **segments** upper layer protocols

- The Transport Layer helps to **hides details** from the upper layers by providing **transparent data transfer**

- The Transport Layer's **flow control** mechanism helps to prevent data from overwhelming the destination node

- The Transport Layer also utilizes an **acknowledgement** system whereby a source node will wait for a random period of time to receive an acknowledgement *(Ack)* from the destination node

- The Transport Layer uses **windowing** to control the flow of packets. Windowing specifies how much data can be transmitted. The best window size is **number 3**

- The Transport Layer transmits segments error-free *(error correction)*

- The Transport Layer performs **sequencing** for error recovery

- The Transport Layer is deemed as **a reliable end-to-end** communication process from the **beginning to the final** transmission

Key terms

Sequencing, acknowledgements, sliding windows, reassembling of data,

UDP, TCP, SPX, flow control, error checking and recovery

NOTE:

Transport Layer = error **correction** prior to retransmitting the packet

Data-Link Layer = error **detection**. No correction

An Overview of Port Numbers

- The Transport Layer uses **Port** Numbers to track and **manage segments**

TCP/IP and UDP port numbers	
public applications	255 and below
proprietary applications	256 – 1023
dynamic usage by hosts application and registered port numbers	1024 and above

256-1023 are also referred as "Well Known Port Numbers"

TCP and UDP randomly select port numbers above 1024 to establish a communication link

NOTE:

The Transport Layer does not use hardware address or flat address.

The Transport Layer uses the MAC address of a NIC card

Other Port Numbers			
Telnet	=	23	
FTP	=	20,	21
SMTP	=	161,	162
SNMP	=	25	
HTTP	=	80	
DNS	=	53	

An Overview of Flow Control

Flow control can also be achieved with **Ready/Ready Not codes**

Flow control uses Windowing, Buffering, and Source-quench messages

Windowing is the amount of data that is predetermined before an acknowledgement *(Ack)* is sent. If the sent acknowledgement is not received, then the data is resent

Buffering is the temporary storage of data in the **memory buffers** until they can be processed. If the buffers are full, the excess data packets are discarded. However, when the sender is notified about the discarded frames, the sender retransmits them to the destination address.

Source-quench messages: When the buffers are full, a message is sent from the destination area to tell the source area that its **device memory** is full and to slow down its data transmission rate.

NOTE:

Windowing is also referred to as Sliding Windows

Set its parameter number to 3

RTMP resides in AppleTalk's Transport Layer. It is a flow control process that is responsible for establishing and maintaining the routing tables.

NSP is a DECnet Transport Layer Protocol that is responsible for its flow control.

An Overview of Connection-Oriented Services

The Transport Layer functions with TCP, UDP and SPX packets.

TCP	Transmission Control Protocol	connection-oriented, guaranteed. FTP uses TCP
NBP	Name Binding Protocol	AppleTalk. Maps network-visible entities (NVE) with the network address
UDP	User Datagram Protocol	best effort, connectionless. TFTP uses UDP
SPX	Sequenced Packet Exchange	Novell's proprietary connection-oriented protocol, reliable

- TCP provides flow control and error checking and correction

- TCP is a reliable, full-duplex **stream** services that is connection-oriented

- TCP provides connection-oriented services to **create a virtual circuit**

- UDP provides connectionless datagram service

- The Transport Layer TCP/IP function provides connection-oriented services

- The Transport Layer has the ability to work with **multiple** applications under a single transport and **multiplexing** of the upper-layer applications

- The Transport Layer helps to **tear down** virtual circuits

Problems with Connection-Oriented Data Transmissions

- It requires a virtual circuit

- It must create a static-path selection and static reservation of network resources

NOTE:

Frame Relay, X.25, and ATM

are also considered to be connection-oriented

even though they do not utilize error-checking capabilities

Network Layer

Level 3

- The Network Layer manages the addressing, tracking, and the pointing of devices through internetworks

- The Network Layer helps to **selects the appropriate path** for the packet to get to its destination

- Packets and Protocols work hand-in-hand in the Network Layer with its associated PDU

- The two key functions of the Network Layer are **path determination and packet switching**

- Network topology consists of: Token Ring, Ethernet, Token-Bus, MESH

- The Network Layer permits **multiple data links** to be combined into an internetwork through **logical addressing** schemes.

*Logical addresses are also referred to as **Protocol addresses***

- The Network Layer moves data. **It forwards the data**

- **Routing** occurs at the Network Layer

Key Words

IP, IPX, ARP, logical addressing, forwards the packets,
path determination and path selection, ICMP

To verify a Network Layer's connectivity between

two devices

Router#ping [ip address]

An Overview of Network Protocols

BGP	Border Gateway Protocol	exterior protocol, replaces EGP
IP	Internet Protocol	TCP/IP Suite, hierarchal logical addressing; **connectionless**, unreliable, depends on TCP
ARP	Address Resolution Protocol	maps and resolves **IP** addresses to MAC addresses
RARP	Reverse Address Resolution Protocol	maps and resolves **MAC** addresses to IP addresses
ICMP	Internet Control Message Protocol	uses Ping, Telnet, and Trace to check connectivity issues. Destination Unreachable is the most common error message
OSPF	Open Shortest Path First	Link-State Protocol. Uses LSA
RIP	Routing Information Protocol	Distance Vector Protocol
IPX	Internet Packet Exchange	Netware Protocol, **best effort**
NLSP	NetWare Link Services Protocol	default for NetWare 4.11 +
DDR	Datagram Delivery Protocol	AppleTalk's method of path determination based on cost
AARP	AppleTalk Address Resolution Protocol	maps network addresses to hardware addresses
DRP	DECnet Routing Protocol	SUN Microsystems DECnet Phase IV usage

The reference wordings on the ARP and RARP can get confusing.
There are also references to known MAC and known IP.

*IP to a **known** MAC = ARP*

*MAC to a **known** IP = RAPR*

An Overview of Packets and Datagrams

- A packet can be **compressed** by the Network Layer

- The Network Layer is responsible for **data transfer** across the network and the **routing of IP messages**

Hierarchical addressing relies on logically structured address – IP address

- The Network Layer uses **logical** hierarchical addresses

Through IP   or   IPX

NOTE:

(Even though IPX is a Network Layer, it is not under the

usage of the IP Protocol.

IPX is it own entity.)

Don't forget: ARP and RARP are Network 3 Layers

Quick Reference Tool
packets = Network Layer
Network Layer = ICMP

An Overview of Routers

- The Network Layer DOES NOT use flat or hardware address

*The Data-Link layer contains flat or hardware address
in their Switches and Bridges*
whereas
*Routers reside and operate at the Network Layer and can use
dynamic and static addressing schemes*

- The router's major function is to transfer packets from one network to another

- Routers are programmed to make decisions concerning the flow of packets

- Routers create and maintain routing tables

metric information resides inside the routing table

NOTE:

The Network Layer also **supports multiplexing**
as the routers require the ability to forward their packets
to many different interfaces

An Overview of Data-Link WAN Protocols

Level 2

SDLC	Synchronous Data-Link Protocol is a communication protocol. Circuit switched / Packet switched, bit-oriented, **Full-Duplex** and half-duplex serial protocol, point-to-point/multipoint links
HDLC	High Level Data-Link Control Protocol is a bit-oriented synchronous protocol that derived from SDLC. HDLC specifies a **data-encapsulation** method on synchronous **serial links** using frame characters and checksums. Also, HDLC is the **default encapsulation on point-to-point links** between Cisco routers Use HDLC when you configure two routers for a point-to-point synchronous serial link on a WAN *(same as peer-to-peer)*
ISDN	Integrated Services Digital Network is a protocol that allows telephone companies *(telco)* to carry **data, voice and video.** ISDN is a circuit switching protocol that uses digital telephone lines. **Q.921** and **Q-931** works under the Q reference
Frame Relay	Handles **multiple virtual-circuits** by using the HDLC encapsulation method between connected devices. Replaces X.25. Can use **IEFT encapsulation or Cisco (default)**
LAPB	Link Access Procedure, Balance is a bit-oriented protocol derived from HDLC. Associated also with PPP
X.25	A packet-switched, **connection-oriented** protocol that uses LCNs to distinguish the connections between the DTEs at their end-points.

HDLC and ISDN can also use the Network layer

PPP	Point-to-Point is the successor to SLIP. Provides router-to-router and host-to-network connections over **synchronous and asynchronous** circuits.
SMDS	Switched Multimegabit Data Service is a high-speed, packet switched, datagram service offered by the telephone company.
SIP, Level 3 and 2	SMDS Interface Protocol is used to communicate between CPE *(Customer Premise Equipment)* and SMDS network equipment. SIP allows the CPE to use SMDS services. SIP Level 3 and 2 reside at the MAC layer. SIP Level 1 resides at the Physical Layer and works with DS-1 and DS-3 lines to create a communication link between the DPE devices in the network cloud. IEEE **802.6**
X.25	A packet-switching protocol. Uses SVC for a temporary connection on a as need basis. The QLCC uses X.25 to transport SNA data across the X.25 network. X-121 is its addressing standard.
CPE	Customer Premises Equipment. Terminals, telephones, and modems that are supplied by the telephone company at the customer's site and connected to the telephone company's network, usually in a closet, which is referred to as the **Demarc**.
CDP	Cisco Discovery Protocol runs on Cisco routers, access servers, and switches. CDP uses discovery methods to exchange data. **Enabled by default**.
SNAP	Subnetwork Access Protocol is used to gather information about router's **directly connected** neighbors.

These LAN Protocols are also a part of the Data-Link Protocol
Ethernet
FDDI
Token-Ring
Fast Ethernet

An Overview of Data Link's Physical Addressing

The Data Link layer performs physical addressing in the form of a MAC address

- The Data-Link **uses the physical addresses** of a NIC card (Network Adapter Card) to forward a frame.

- The Data Link layer encapsulates packets from the upper layers into frames

- Each frame is addressed in the header with the source and destination address

- The Data-Link layer synchronizes transmission and handles error correction

*The Data Link Layer uses **CRC** [cyclical redundancy check]*
for error notification

- The Data-Link layer Provides **reliable transmission of data** across a *physical medium*

- The Data-Link layer performs the **conversion of data into bits** for transmission over physical media

Don't confuse this with the Physical Layer function which is used to transport bits inside the wire

Quick Reference Note
Network Layer = logical addressing
Data-Link Layer = physical addressing
Transport Layer = data segmenting

- The MAC Address uses **physical addressing** to discover the device under IEEE regulations

- The MAC address is created to deliver a packet to the end device

- The MAC's node address is 48 bits long and is composed of a vendor code (24 bits) and a serial number (24 bits) that is burned into the Network Interface Card

- The MAC's network address is 32 bits long

The first 6 hexadecimal digits of the MAC address is called the OUI
Each NIC card has its own unique number.
This Burned In Address (BIA) is placed in the EEPROM by the vendor

- A MAC address is assigned to a LAN interface through a **Bridge**.

A Bridge can filter traffic based on the MAC address NOT by the IP address

IP addresses are forwarded by routers

Bridges pass broadcast traffic to all ports

The MAC address is also called a physical address as well as a NIC Address

Examples of Physical addresses

IP

139.123.45.6
For IP: the network ID is 139.123.45. The Host ID is 6

IPX

9a.1234.5678.9AB3
For IPX: the network ID is 9a while the IPX the node address is 1234.5678.9AB3

IPX = 32 bits for the network address. And, 48 bits for the node address portion

Hexadecimal numbers work like this. A decimal 10 = the letter A.

B = 11. C = 12. D = 13. E = 14. F = 15.
9AB3 is the same as 9,10,11,3

- When the Data Link Layer performs the sequencing of frames, it puts 1's and 0's into a logical group

An Overview of Data Link's
MAC Sublayer

Media Access Control

- When you need to **access the protocols** that work within the **Physical** network areas, you must use the MAC Sublayer

- The MAC Sublayer will permit you to identify **multiple devices** that reside on the Data-Link layer. To perform this task, the MAC layer utilizes MAC addressing schemes. Of course, each address is unique (one of a kind).

- The MAC Sublayer **manages protocol access** to the physical network medium

Don't confuse this stuff with the Network Layer stuff

NOTE:

Concerning 1's and 0's

One of the confusing areas with the Data-Link Layer and the Physical Layer
is the usage of 1's and 0's. Both layers utilize the usage of ones and zeros.

To distinguish the difference, use this formula:

The Physical layer = 1's and 0s' in the **wire**

whereas

The Data-Link layer = 1's and 0's in the **Frame**

An Overview of Data Link's LLC Sublayer

Logical Link Control

- The LLC Layer is a Data Link Sublayer under IEEE 802.2. The LLC Sublayer provides the support basis for **unacknowledged connectionless** services and for **connection-oriented** services on the Local Area Network (LAN).

  This is referred as a Class I device, Type 1

- The Logical Link Control Sublayer **manages communications** between devices over a single link of a network through a flow control mechanism

- CDP's **SNAP** frame functions under LLC

- The LLC Sublayer supports **connection-oriented** protocols

This is referred as Type 2, or LLC 2, and works with Class II devices

- The LLC Sublayer supports connectionless protocols

  This is referred as Type 3, Class III device

A Class IV device can support all three types of LCC services

- LLC Sublayer uses Service Access Points (**SAP**) to interact with the upper-layer protocols

LLC uses the DSAP and the SSAP of the frame = AA

- LLC Sublayer **operates independently** of the other protocols

It is really easy to falsely combine this knowledge with the Network Layer.

The LLC Sublayer shares common terms with the Network Layer,
so you must be careful to learn
the differences between them.

Think in terms of frames and SAPs

An Overview of how the Data-Link Layer Works with Bridges and Switches

- Bridges and Switches operate at the Data Link layer (Layer 2)

- Bridges filter traffic based on a MAC address

- To prevent potential loops Bridges and Switches use the **Spanning Tree Protocol**

The Spanning Tree Protocol works in this order: blocking, listening, learning, and forwarding.

The STP uses the Spanning Tree Algorithm

*The SPA is also referred as IEEE **802.1d***

The Physical layer does not use hardware or flat address. It only transmits bits over the physical media

**** The Data link layer contains flat and hardware address ****

- The Data Link layer selects the appropriate path that a packet should take to reach the destination through the Bridge or Switch

- The Data Link layer *transports data* across a physical link with a Bridge or a Switch

NOTE:

LAN Switching is a Data-Link Layer process

Physical Layer

Level 1

- The Physical Layer concerns itself with **electrical** and **mechanical** functions

- The Physical Layer works with **voltage level** specifications, the timing of voltage changes, and the speed and distance of the physical data rate exchange process

- The Physical layer activates, maintains, and deactivates the physical link between end systems

- The Physical Layer sets standards for cabling's maximum **transmission distances** and the associated physical connection **device hardware** – the physical **components** that are to be used with the cabling

  RJ-45, EIA/TIA 232, transceiver, etc

  The V.35 uses 34 pins

- Network Interface Cards *(NICs)* reside at the Physical layer

- The Physical Layer concerns itself with the bit synchronization of 1's and 0's on the wire

NOTE:

Protocols are specified as software at the Physical Layer

RS-235 is the same as EIA/TIA 235

Don't forget: SIP Level 1 resides in the Physical Layer

An Overview of HSSI
(High-Speed Serial Interface Protocol)

- HSSI is utilized by the Physical Layer

- HSSI is a WAN protocol

- HSSI corresponds to the Physical layer. Its maximum cable length is 50 feet, and HSSI transmits at 52Mbps. HSSI is used as a DTE/DCE interface

- HSSI uses a 100BaseT4 Unshielded Twisted Pair (UTP) wire for voice transmission over Fast Ethernet

HSSI can handle a T3 transmission – 45Mbps

HSSI must be set up on a point-to-point topology basis

- HSSI can be used as a high speed connector between Ethernet and Token Ring

HSSI LOOPBACK TEST PARAMETERS

1 **Cable test:** the signal loops back after it reaches the DTE port

2 **DCE test:** checks the local DCE

3 **Telco line test:** checks the remote DCE through a WAN link

4 **DTE test:** the local DCE checks on the transmitting DTE, then the transmitting DTE replies to the local DCE that it is operational

HSSI's Peer-Based Communication requires two signals. The first one is used to indicate that the DTE is available. The second signal indicates that the DCE is also available. The HSSI's Peer-Based Communication connection **assumes intelligence** in the DCE and DTE devices.

The ECL (emitter-coupled logic) is used by HSSI to achieve a high data-transferring rate along with a low noise level. The ECL permits reliable timing and retiming standards

HSSI uses a 50 pin male-to-male connector (similar to SCSI-2's connector)

An Overview of Cabling Criteria

The Physical Layer sends data over these physical medium:

Ethernet

802.3 = CSMA/CA

Default on Netware 3.11, also known as novell-ether

NetWare 4.11 uses SAP as its default encapsulation

- 10Base2 = thinnet, 185 meters or 607 feet, max of 30 PCs, printers, repeaters

- 10Base5 = thicknet, is a Bus topology that has a maximum useful length of 500 meters or 1,640 feet. It can work with a maximum of 100 nodes

- 10BaseT uses unshielded twisted pair cabling: Cat 3, 4, 5 connected to a RJ-45. It works up to 100 meters or 328 feet.

- 100BaseT has a maximum length of 100 meters or 328 feet; and works with a maximum of 1,024 nodes. 100BaseT uses a two-pair Cat 5 cable. 100BaseT works with CSMA/CD and IEEE **802.3u** *(Fast Ethernet)*

- 100BaseFx is also known as a point-to-point ethernet topology. 100BaseFx works up to 400 meters

- Hubs, repeaters, transceivers, operate at the Physical Layer

NOTE:

10BaseT and 100BaseTx are configured in a Star topology.

Token Ring & Fast Ethernet

(802.5)

- Type 1 STP cable, 101 meters or 331 feet, max of 260 nodes

- Type 3 UTP cable, 45 meters or 148 feet, max of 72 nodes

Fast Ethernet

- Fast Ethernet is implemented at the **Core and Distribution** layers of a campus LAN.

10BaseT acts as the Access layer for Fast Ethernet

- 100BaseT uses a Cat 5, two-pair cable, with a RJ-45 connector

- 100BaseT4 uses a Cat 3, four-pair cable, with a RJ-45 connector

- 100BaseFx uses a micron multimode fiber comprised of 2 strands and uses a Duplex metric-interface connector *(MIC)*

- When the 100BaseFx cable is connected between the DTE and the DCE it can transmit up to 400 meters.

100 VG-AnyLAN & FDDI

100 Dedication

To my wife who lost many hours of sleep trying to keep up with all the things that interest me.

One day soon, the time will come when our hands will embrace and hold gently throughout the afternoon.

IEEE 802.12

- 100VG-AnyLAN uses a 4 pair Cat 3 UTP cable, or a 2 pair Cat 4 and 5 UTP, or a STP, or fiber optic

- 100VG-AnyLAN is used for time-sensitive applications such as multimedia

- 100VG-AnyLAN access methodology is referred to as demand-priority, and has a transmission speed of 16Mbps in a Token Ring environment

FDDI

(ANSI X3T9.5)

- FDDI uses fiber-optic cabling that transmits at 100Mbps. FDDI uses Token passing. It's topology is set up as a dual-ring that utilizes counter-rotating exchanges. The FDDI is effective up to a length of 2 kilometers and can have a maximum of 100 nodes

- **Autonegotiation** enables a device and a hub to exchange information through a 100BaseT cable and incorporates FLP (pulses) that creates automatic signaling in the 100BaseT4 station.

An Overview of IEEE Specifications

802.1	internetwork
802.1d	Spanning Tree Protocol
802.1q	VLAN trunking protocol
802.2	logical link control
802.3	**CSMA/CD (ethernet)**
802.3u	Fast Ethernet
802.3z	Gigabit Ethernet: (fiber & copper)
802.3ab	Gigabit Ethernet (UTP)
802.4	Token Bus
802.5	Token Ring
802.6	Metropolitan Area Networking, SIP, DQDB
802.7	Broadband technology
802.8	Fiber-optic technology
802.9	ISDN
802.10	Networking security, and VLAN identifiers that can be carried within FDDI network traffic
802.11	Wireless networking
802.12	100BaseVG-AnyLAN

Startup Sequence

When the router is first turned on it will look for the IOS software in NVRAM. If the IOS is not there, it will look next in flash. If absent from there, it will proceed to the TFTP server. The fourth step is for the router outer to look at the **ROM monitor mode**. ROM is defined as the place of **last resort** for the router to load its IOS from.

1. The Bootstrap program in ROM executes POST. The bootstrap program can also boot from a TFTP server or flash *(image)*

2. The IOS is loaded into memory from the boot system command

3. The configuration file is loaded into memory from NVRAM

• If no configuration file is found in any of the four steps, then the setup program of the IOS will initiate the **setup** dialog

square brackets [ ] have default and optional answers that follow a yes / no question

ctrl + c terminates the setup process

To setup from the Exec Mode, type
    Router#setup

After you have logged on, you are placed in **User mode**
    Router>

To enter the Privileged mode, type **enable** after >
    Router>enable

The **>** will change to **#**
    Router#

Then type config t after Router#
    Router#config t

> *config t is used to modify and view configuration*
> *files*
> *and the IOS parameters in a router*

The order of a router search for the boot system command are

NVRAM, Flash, Network

To boot a router from a TFTP server

Router(config)#boot system tftp [configuration-file-name] [tftp-server-address]

Or

Router(config)#boot system tftp BeMyBaby.bin 123.45.67.1

To boot from an IOS located on a remote TFTP server

Router(config)#boot system tftp IOS.exe [ip address]

The router can also boot from a DECnet MOP server,
from a server through RCP, and of course,
from a tftp filename or from a tftp URL.

And, in case you want to go exotic and have the best, the latest and the greatest IOS file image upgrade, type in

Router#copy tftp flash

Or

Router#copy [source | destination]

The IOS image file has five parts to it

1   the **platform** that runs the image

2   the special **capabilities** of the image file

3   where the image files runs and if it is **compressed**

4   the IOS image **version** number

5   and the file **extension**

Start-Up Scenario

When you type
    Router#show protocols
Or at the console terminal you type
Router#show interface s1   *(or e1, e0, s0)*
and you receive this message, it means:

Serial1 is down, line protocol is down
It means that the cable is physically disconnected

Serial1 is administratively down, line protocol is down
the administrator manually disabled the interface

Serial1 is up, line protocol is down
There are no keepalives, no clock rate, the wrong connector, or you have a back-to-back connection. Or, the other end of the connection is administratively down.

A back-to-back connection does not use a modem, and both routers are acting as the DCE devices

DCE devices provides the clocking signal

To turn on the interface
    Router#no shutdown

NOTE:

Ethernet is a part of the Physical layer

Line protocol is a part of the Data-Link layer

Flash Memory

- Flash memory is an erasable, reprogramable type of ROM memory.

- Flash memory retains **Images** of the operating system and the router's **microcode**

- Flash memory can be **upgraded / programmed** without replacing the chips

- Flash memory can have more than one operating system, if enough memory space is available

- Flash memory stores copies of the router's configuration file

- Flash memory is **used by TFTP** when implementing the transfer of an operating system *(IOS)* to another router

- You do not have to replace the Flash memory chip as you do ROM's chips

Cisco's IOS can also be loaded from flash memory,
or from ROM,
or from a network location = TFTP server,
during the startup sequence

The Router#show flash

displays the name of the system image file,
the total amount of memory, and the
available memory left to work with to load another IOS

Flash memory holds the IOS image file

In other words: flash memory contains the IOS

If no image is found in flash, the router goes to ROM

To load an IOS file from flash memory
Router#boot system flash [IOS filename]

This Command Line Interface permits the first flash file to
be discovered by the router inside flash to be loaded on the
next bootup of the router.

The configuration-register parameter of the bootup file in
NVRAM's flash is 0x2 – 0x2F

ROM

- Read Only Memory is a physical chip on a router's motherboard that contains the router's **bootstrap** program

- You need to remove and replace the ROM chips if any modifications are needed

- ROM contains code that performs power-on diagnostics similar to power-on self test (POST) that many PC's perform.

Only ROM executes POST.

POST performs the hardware-level check

ROM contains the operating system

so does flash memory and the tftp sever from a remote location

<hr>

To improve performance of the router add more memory in RAM

Upgrading ROM with a new chip does not improve a router's performance

To load the IOS from ROM
Router#boot system rom

*The boot system in ROM is used as the **last resort** method to boot the router*

First, use flash memory to find the operating system. If flash does not contain the operating system, go to the TFTP server.

Finally, use the last resort method:
Router#boot system ROM

RAM

- RAM holds routing tables

- RAM performs packet buffering

- RAM queues packets

- RAM provides memory for the router's configuration file when the device is operational

- RAM holds the ARP cache and IP addressing information

When powered down, ALL the contents are lost

To copy the startup configuration file in NVRAM **to** the running configuration in RAM

 Router#copy startup-config running-config

This is the same as saying

To load the router configuration into RAM
Router#copy start run

To copy the running configuration **from** RAM to tftp server
 Router#copy running-config tftp

To copy the startup configuration file in NVRAM to a tftp server

Router#copy startup-config tftp

Be careful not to confuse this with NVRAM

To load the router configuration into RAM from a TFTP server

Router#copy tftp run

Summary of Functions	
Flash	Contains the IOS
RAM	dynamic memory, contains the running configuration file and the **currently active** configuration files
ROM	Boot Strap Code and POST
NVRAM	Contains the **backup** configuration file

NOTE:

On initial startup and set-up, the IOS will use both RAM and NVRAM.
This is the only instance where both functions are used by the IOS

RAM = running configuration

You can configure the running-configuration *(RAM)*
1   from the console terminal,
2   from the tftp server *(also called the network)*
3   and from NVRAM *(also referred to as memory)*

**To improve the performance of the router
add more memory in RAM**

You have to replace the chips in ROM,
and that may not improve its performance

RAM serves as the main memory area of the router that stores programs and the Cisco IOS. Remember, RAM cannot permanently store information. so when the pouter is powered off, the information is lost.

To see the configuration file in RAM
    Router#show running-config
Or
    Router#show version

*The buffer stores the packets when the
router's memory is overloaded*

To review RAM
    Router#show protocols
                    Or
    Router#show version
                    Or
    Router#show running-config

The running-config displays the running configuration file to a console terminal

NVRAM

Nonvolatile Read Access Memory

- NVRAM keeps it contents when the power is turned off

- NVRAM **stores** the startup or running configuration file, allowing the router to quickly recover from a power failure

It is always a good idea to use an Uninterrupted Power Supply - UPS

- NVRAM does not need a hard disk or floppy for the configuration file

You should store your configuration files on a PC, so when you do need to modify your files, you can use the PC's text editor

You can load directly to the router's NVRAM by using the TFTP via the network

You will need tftp server software when the router becomes the client and the computer becomes the server

To copy the saved configuration to a TFTP server
>   Router#copy nvram tftp

To **view** the **configuration file** stored in NVRAM
>   Router#sh run

Or
>   Router#show running

Or
>   Router#show running-config

afterwards, press any key on the keyboard to return to
Router#

> *These three are the displays commands to examine the*
> *configuration file.*
> *They are not the copy, load, backup, or review command*

To review the **contents** of NVRAM
and
To display the router's **backup** configuration file from NVRAM

    Router#show config

Or

    Router#show startup-config

Attributes
NVRAM contains the backup configuration file NVRAM = startup-config
RAM contains the active configuration file RAM = running config

Command Line Interfaces	
RAM	NVRAM
show config	show protocol
show running-config	show version
	show startup-config

To erase or delete the startup config from NVRAM

    Router#erase startup-config

To save a configuration to NVRAM
Or
To copy the running configuration file in RAM to the startup configuration file in NVRAM

> Router#copy run start   *and press enter*
> Or
> Router#copy running   *and press the tab key*
> Or
> Router#copy running-config startup-config   *and press*
enter

To **execute** the configuration stored in NVRAM use the **configure memory** argument
> Router#config-mem

To copy the startup configuration file **in** NVRAM **to** a tftp server
Or
To copy the router's configuration **from** NVRAM to a file server
> Router#copy startup-config tftp

Be careful not to confuse this with RAM

Router#copy running-config tftp
*copies the running configuration file **from** RAM to a tftp server*

NVRAM does not affect the performance of running programs

NVRAM does NOT store the IOS

ROM contains the IOS!

NOTE:

NVRAM, in one special instance (the initial startup of the router) will store
the startup configuration (NVRAM) and the running configuration files (RAM)

in = from

Routing Metrics

The routing metric is a routing algorithm that determines that one route is better than another. Information is stored in the routing table.

Metrics include

- Communication cost
- Delay
- Load
- Hop count
- Path cost
- Reliability
- MTU

Maximum Transmission Unit is a packet size that a particular interface can handle

MTU is measured in bytes.

The Routing Protocols

- Routing protocols **moves data** through paths in a network

- The Routing Protocols work on **path determination**

Some of the Routing Protocols are

BGP, OSPF, IGRP, EIGRP,
IP RIP, IPX RIP, NLSP,
RTMP,
Vinnes VTP, IS-IS, SNA Routing,
IP Multicast,
NLSP, OSI ES-IS, IDRP

NOTE:

The Routed Protocols concern themselves with addressing issues
whereas
The Routing Protocols are concerned with the topology and data changes

A router relies on the Routing Protocols to forward the data

Key Terms

IGRP and RIP are referred to as classful routing protocols. These two do not forward subnet addressing schemes

To establish the routing protocols on an optimal path algorithm, use

Router#passive interface [type number]

The passive interface listens for RIP and IGRP advertisements about the connected subnet, but the passive interface does not send updates on its interface, with the exception of the e1 interface.

Routed Protocols

Some of the Routed Protocols are:

TCP/IP, CLNP, DECnet, AppleTalk (AARP),

Old Vinnes, and Banyan Vinnes,

SNA

The Internet Protocols (IP, TCP, UDP, ICMP, ARP, RARP),

NetWare (IPX, SPX)

XNS, and OSI Protocols

These Protocols are also referred to as Network Protocols

Routable Protocols contain network layer addressing

IP RIP

Routing Information Protocol

Administrative Distance 120

RIP is a **dynamic** routing protocol that has its entries entered automatically by the router

*To do this the router uses a **routing** protocol*

To enable RIP on an IP and have it advertise that network
    Router#config t
    Router(config)#router rip
    Router(config-router)#network [ip address]
    Router(config-router)^Z
    Router#

It is important to know that an ip address is required on the network line

RIP can also utilize an Administrative Number in its Command Line configuration

- RIP is a Distance Vector protocol.

- RIP updates topology changes every 30 seconds = slow convergence

- RIP has a maximum of 15 hops. The 16th is considered **unreachable**

IP RIP uses only hop count *(bandwidth based)* as a routing metric,
whereas
IPX RIP uses tick meter count, in addition to hop count

The media must be identical, otherwise RIP will fail to perform

To see RIP information on the router's network

Router#show ip protocol

Or

Router#debug ip rip

When you are working with RIP you will eventually encounter several unpleasant occurrences. To overcome the shortcomings and the impact of the RIP protocol counting to infinity and its nasty habit of creating routing loops, you must incorporate several preventive scopes in your router.

To prevent the problem of looping in Distance Vector Protocols use	
route poisoning	makes the route unreachable
split horizon	does not return the information learned from the original source (Frame Relay and NBMA uses this as well)
maximum hop-count	15 max hops with RIP 255 max hops with IGRP
holddowns	ignores the network updates for a specified amount of time
triggered updates	is actually used for preventive maintenance. It notifies the router whenever a topology change occurs in the network

IP RIP applications are: DNS, SMTP, and Telnet

NOTE:

RIP and IGRP do not support Variable Length Subnet Masks

RIP, version 2 does support VLSM

RIP and IGRP are classful protocols

Use ip classless when configuring

To see the RIP incoming and outgoing RIP updates
Or
To see the RIP routes entering and leaving the router
Router#debug ip rip

To prevent routing loops in IP RIP and to reduce
the occurrence and impact of counting to infinity, use

1   **Split horizon:** This will speed up convergence. It will never return information back to the originating sender. Some ex-wives should be like this.

The problem with slow convergence is that it may create an inconsistent path to the destination

2   **route poisoning:** An inconsistent update will play havoc with your router. Old information is not good information. The router requires consistent updates that are correct. The routing table entry will help the router to converge to a new topology with everything in its proper place. Incorrect updates have no place in our routers. Our gossiping friends should be poisoned in such fashion.

Use with hold-down timers

3   **hold-down timers:** This prevents a regular update message from reinstalling a bad routing path. The router will remain down for a period of time exceeding the necessary time required to correct the bad path. The hold down timer will mark a route as inaccessible and will search for a better metric. When it is found, the hold-down timer status is

removed. The timer will also be reset after a triggered update has expired or if another update message is received telling the router that the network has changed. I could use this guide in my life. Hold back! Hold back! Ok, it's now safe to go on.

4 **maximum hop count:** This will stop the packets from endlessly looping around the network in search of a device to say hello to. Some of our lives may loop endlessly, but that should not be the case with our packets. So, unlike our lives, we can prevent that endless treachery by manually saying no after the fifteenth attempt of trying to say hello to someone. Just corrupt the thing by manually placing a 16th incremental hop count to the information bank. Bang, the darn packet freezes in its track and all is safe.

NOTE:

The most effective means to solve the
"count to infinity" problem
is to utilize the "**Defining a Maximum**" parameter

- **Router#sh ip route** shows the **routes** and the **contents** of an ip routing table that were learned by RIP, and the static routes known to the router as well as the directly connected routes, *(dynamic)*.

- **Router#sh ip protocol** displays the information about RIP **timer values** and the network on which RIP is configured, and the **gateway** used by RIP to gain information, and the **routing protocol parameters**, and the rate at which updates occur, and the amount of time before the next update will be sent from the router.

- **Router#debug ip rip** is used to display RIP **routing updates** as they occur. The command includes routing updates that are broadcast and received by the router.

So, to summarize

- RIP measures by using the hop count from the originating source to the final destination router.

- RIP updates every **30** seconds whereas IPX RIP updates every **60** seconds

(IGRP = 90 seconds)

- RIP has a default of **4 equal cost paths** when it performs its load-balance

You can go up to 6 equal cost paths

- RIP has an **Administrative Distance** trustworthiness of 120

Reverse thinking here. The most trusted is a flat zero
"Sir, on a basis of 0 – 10, how much do you trust her?"
"Why, I trust her zero."
Which of course means you trust her the most.

- RIP is also an **unsecure** protocol. Because RIP only uses fixed metrics you cannot use it in a large network where you need to establish real-time parameters, load, and reliability. Use OSPF for that kind of security.

RIP will not support VLSM
(Variable length Subnet Masks)
that are used in variable subnetting.

Use OSPF. RIPv2 will support VLSM.

IP Multicast

In an IP multicast environment, a single packet is sent to a multicast group, which is identified by a single IP destination address

This single IP packet can be sent simultaneously to multiple hosts.

IP Multicast uses IGMP (Internet Group-Membership Protocol) for the creation of multicast groups. IGMP works only with a Class D address (224-239).

IP Multicast relies on the usage of PIM (Protocol-Independent Multicast). PIM uses reverse path flooding for its data-stream transmission

IP Multicast also uses MOSPF (Multicast Open Shortest Path First) which uses a unicast routing protocol to become aware of the transmitting links. MOSPF calculates these routers for the source. MOSPF only works with OSPF.

IPX RIP

You must enable RIP on an IPX network
whereas
RIP is enabled by default on IP

IPX RIP uses delay and ticks to determine its next metric destination.
IP RIP only uses hop count.

To enable IPX RIP on your router:
    Router#config t
    Router(config)#ipx routing
    Router(config-**ipx**-router)#^Z

*After you establish the configuration command line,
it will have **ipx** within the parenthesis*

To encapsulate IPX type:
    Router#config t
    Router(config)#ipx routing
    Router(config)#int e0
    Router(config-if)#ipx network 20 encapsulation sap
    Router(config-if)#^Z

To add a secondary IPX network add the work "**sec**" after "sap" encapsulate:
Router(config-if)#ipx network 20 encapsulation sap **sec**

sec is shorthand for "secondary"

RIP and IGRP contains their argument after the word router within their parameter.
IPX is reverse. It has ipx in front of the word routing

Router(config)#router rip versus Router(config)#ipx routing

IPX RIP uses novell-ether as its default encapsulation

IPX RIP supports multiple paths through the usage of
Router(config)#ipx maximum paths [#]   *(up to 6)*

To verify an IPX route
Router#sh ipx route

Distance-Vector Vs Link State

Distance-Vector Problems

A Distance-Vector Protocol is useful only in a small network. It can develop routing loops, and the packets that is trying to transmit, can get stuck in a counting bind eternally. (I suppose – as no one ever invented an eternal computer. I've always laughed whenever Captain Piccard of Star Trek said to Data: "Why, this computer must be at least 200,000 years old! Doesn't anyone remember "continental drift"?)

Distance-Vector also suffers from slow convergence. It's insistence on constant periodic updates contributes greatly to this occurrence, and effects convergence times, which, of course, are significantly slower.

Each router that uses the Distance-Vector Protocol is compelled to send all or a part of their routing table of their neighbors. Friendly, aren't they?

Link State Protocol

The router that incorporates a Link-State Protocol converges faster. They avoid routing loops, but they require more CPU processing and memory usage. You see, their eyes never close.

Link-State Protocols are **more expensive** than Distance-Vector.

Open Shortest Path First

Administrative Distance 110

- OSPF is a Link-State **Routing** Protocol that uses LSP (Link State Packets) to inform other routers of distant links

OSPF sends the state of its links to all routers in its domain

- OSPF triggers an update when the topology changes. This decreases bandwidth usage.

OSPF converges faster than RIP or IGRP

- OSPF analyzes bandwidth and network congestion whenever it makes a routing decision

OSPF maintains a more complex Forwarding and Routing Table than RIP

- OSPF is a hierarchical routing algorithm proposed as a successor to RIP in the internet community.

OSPF uses least-cost routing, multiple routing, and load balancing

- OSPF is derived from the IS-IS protocol

- OSPF can partition an Autonomous System (AS) into logical areas

- OSPF does not use a hop count metric so there is no maximum amount of hops to be concerned with.

- OSPF uses LSA packets instead of broadcasts

Each LSA packet contains the complete Routing Table

- OSPF can use bandwidth as one of its path delay schemes

   OSPF is not limited to a hop count metric

OSPF Problems

- OSPF can flood the network

- OSPF requires more processing power, more bandwidth, more memory to achieve the same throughput as RIP

- Update synchronization can also be a problem

A router uses detailed knowledge of the topology of the network

To mitigate the shortcomings of a link-state protocol

- **Lengthen the update frequency** in order to minimize the router resource usage

- Attach **time-stamps** or sequence numbers on the link-state packets so you can coordinate the updates

- Exchange route summaries

To view OSPF timers
Or
To view configured OSPF areas
     Router#show ip ospf

To view **ALL** OSPF's adjacent routers
     Router#show ip ospf neighbors

Border Gateway Protocol (BGP)

Administrative Distance 20

- BGP is an **exterior** Routing Protocol that is replacing EGP

- BGP communicates reachability, and acts as an interdomain protocol

- BGP guarantees a loop-free exchange of routing information between autonomous systems by working through the TCP/IP suite

  BGP is a connection-oriented protocol

- BGP uses interautonomous system routing, intra-autonomous system routing, and pass-through autonomous system routing

- BGP tables do not require periodic refreshing of its Routing Table because it retains the latest version number of the path it has advertised to its neighbors

Table updates are achieved through incremental updates

- Optimal route is based on the length of the autonomous system's path for a network route

  the shorter, the more trustworthy

- Use BGP when connections have been configured to multiple ISP's to simultaneously forward load balancing and redundancy

To configure BGP on the router
    Router#config t
    Router(config)#router bgp [#]
    Router(config-router)#network [ip address]
    Router(config-router)#^ + Z

NOTE:

Router(config)#router rip works only within a single autonomous system
whereas
Router(config)#router bgp works among different autonomous systems

Exterior Gateway Protocol (EGP)
and Autonomous Systems

- EGP is an exterior internet protocol used to exchange routing information between Autonomous Systems

  An Autonomous System
  is a collection of networks under
  a common administration that shares
  a common routing strategy

- Autonomous Systems are divided by areas.

- You need a unique 16-bit number by the IANA (Internet Assigned Numbers Authority) which delegates authority for IP address space allocation and domain-name assignments by the NIC. IANA maintains the database of assigned protocols identities used in the TCP/IP stack, including AS numbers

- The Autonomous System has a single routing policy

- BGP and EGP protocols help identify the networks that can be reached

- IGRP, EIGRP, OSPF, and NLSP are the routing protocols that use Autonomous System

NLSP = NetWare Link-Services Protocol. It supports
hierarchical addressing

- The Autonomous System has a range from 1-65535

- The routers that use the AS configuration must also be configured with the identical routing protocol

- The routers must be interconnected

- The Routers must use the same AS number to communicate with each other

Interior Gateway Routing Protocol

Administrative Distance 100

- IGRP is a Distance Vector Protocol that utilizes a maximum of 255 hops to discover the route paths to a destination address. OSPF has no hop count

- IGRP is Cisco's designated proprietary protocol

- IGRP uses a T1 line *(1.544Mbps)* on a serial connector on the back of the router

- IGRP can perform **multipath routing**. What does this mean? By incorporating multipath selection, a router can utilize two equal-bandwidth lines to run a single stream of data in **round-robin fashion**. The data will cross over to another line should one become corrupt. The metrics can be different in each line.

- Thus, we can say, IGRP **supports multiple unequal paths** that are configured with an Autonomous Number.

RIP and OSPF support equal paths.

IGRP routers must use the same Autonomous System route to communicate their routes to the each other

- IGRP does not support Variable Length Subnet Masks. **EIGRP does** support VLSM.

- IGRP sends updates every 90 seconds and uses a **composite metric** that involves **bandwidth and delay** parameters by default

To view the **broadcast frequency** of IGRP updates
    Router#sh ip protocols

IGRP, like RIP, uses
Holddowns, Split Horizons and Poison Reverse to solve problems

NOTE:

IGRP advertises interior routes, exterior routes,
and system routes

IGRP's composite metric is composed
of bandwidth and delay

IGRP versus RIP

- IGRP has faster convergence than RIP

- IGRP can work with more multiple paths. IGRP permits a default of 4 **unequal** cost paths between the source and the destination

  IGRP can also scale up to 6 as RIP can

- IGRP works better in a large network = scalability

Time Values		
Processes	*IGRP*	*RIP*
holddown	280 seconds	180 seconds
hop count	255	15
default update timer	90 seconds	30 seconds
invalid route timer	270 seconds	180 seconds
route flush timer	630 seconds	240 seconds

To view the details of an IGRP update messages that are being sent and received

    Router#debug ip igrp transactions

To view IGRP's update summary

    Router#debug ip igrp events

Or

    Router#debug ip igrp [transactions | events]

NOTE:

IGRP and RIP do not support VLSM

IGRP versus OSPF

- IGRP advertises interior routes, system routes, and exterior routes

- OSPF considers hop counts, delay, bandwidth, and reliability when determining the best paths

  IGRP's defaults are delay and bandwidth

- IGRP does not support VLSM. OSPF does support VLSM

To configure IGRP and to provide routing updates for Autonomous System number [#]
    Router#config t
    Router(config)#router igrp [#]
    Router(config-router)#network [ip address]
    Router(config-router)#^ + Z
    Router#

To verify broadcast frequency
    Router#show ip protocol

Enhanced Interior Gateway Routing Protocol

Administrative Distance 90

- EIGRP is a **dynamic** Distance Vector Protocol

  *The preferred term is "**hybrid**" protocol*

- EIGRP uses **integrated multiprotocol routing**: this enables IP, IPX and AppleTalk to share a single protocol instead of three.

(Multiple routed protocols use a common routing protocol)

- Convergence is improved over IGRP

- EIGRP **does support VLSM** and **arbitrary route summarization** / aggregation

RIP and IGRP do not support Variable Length Subnet Mask

- EIGRP advertises its routing table only to neighbor routers that are discovered by the "hello" protocol

EIGRP transmits multicast and unicast packets

- EIGRP selects the least-cost path to a destination and guarantees that the path is not part of a routing loop

- EIGRP parameters: neighbor discovery/recovery scheme, has Reliable Transport Protocol (RTP), and uses protocol-dependent modules.

NOTE:

DUAL finite-state machine selects routes based on feasible successors

To enable EIGRP on a router
    Router#config t
    Router(config)#router eigrp [#]
    Router(config-router)#network [ip address]
    Router(config-router)#^ + Z
    Router#

The brackets indicate an Autonomous number
and the network in the config-router statement requires an
ip address

Advantages of EIGRP

- EIGRP uses hierarchical routing and performs route summarization.

- EIGRP will work with classless routing whereas PPP will not

To view EIGRP's routing table
Router#show ip route eigrp

NOTE:

To permit EIGRP to load balance across unequal paths, use the **variance** command

Comparison of Protocol Time Values

RIP	CDP	IGRP	EIGR
hold down timer 180 seconds	hold time 180 seconds	hold down timer 270 seconds plus 10 seconds = 280 seconds	
hop count 15 max the 16th is considered unreachable		hop count 1-255 hops	hop count 100 hops
default update timers or interval 30 seconds	default update broadcast rate / interval 60 seconds	default update timer or interval 90 seconds	updates are triggered by topology changes
route invalid timer 180 seconds		invalid timer 270 seconds	
route flush timer 240 seconds		flush timer 630 seconds	

Additional Time Information

SAP

- NetWare SAP exchanges information every 60 seconds

- Cisco routers do not forward SAP tables. However, to respond to NetWare's *Get Nearest Sever (GNS)* the router has to listen to the NetWare server's SAP broadcast and record them into their own SAP tables which they do broadcast during their next update

OSPF

- The hop count on OSPF is unlimited

- The updates are triggered by changes

LMI

- Exchanges information with the switch every 10 seconds

VLAN VTP

- Advertises its updates and new information every 5 minutes

Administrative Distances

Static Router	1
BGP	20
EIGRP	90
IGRP	100
OSPF	110
RIP	120

0 is the most trusted

DDR uses an administrative distance of over 200 so it may be chosen last
if more than one router is available

Port Numbers	
TCP	**UDP**
FTP 20, 21	DNS 53
Telnet 23	TFTP 69
SMTP 25	HTTP 80
	SNMP 161, 162

SNMP works with Syslog

DNS = name to IP resolution

Data-Encapsulation

Same as

Peer-to-Peer Communication

Layer	5 Steps of encapsulation	Headers	Process
Application / Session	1. Data		User's **Data** information converted / exchanged to segments
Transport	2. Segments	Transport Header and Data	**Segments** converted / exchanged to packets
Network	3. Packets or Datagrams	Network Header with the logical source and destination address. Also, data	**Packets** converted / exchanged to Frames
Data-Link	4. Frames	Frame Header with the local address	**Frames** are converted / exchanged to bits
Physical	5. Bits	network media transmission	**Bits**

The TCP/IP Data Encapsulation Stack	
Transport	Segment
Network	Packet
Data Link	Frame
Physical	Bits

NOTE:

These protocols talk to each other through the use of PDUs

Five Steps of Data-Encapsulation

The five steps of encapsulation are
Data, Segments, Packets, Frames, Bits

Key

use the last word to know the next step

User starts the encapsulation process. The word user is
paired with the term data

User to data	Application / Session Layer
Data to segment	Transport Layer
Segment to Packets or Datagram	Network Layer
Packets or Datagrams to frames	Data-Link Layer
Frames to bits	Physical Layer

NOTE:

Encapsulation is the process of placing data behind headers
and before the trailers

Data-Encapsulation Order

Another way of remembering the encapsulation order is to write a table

Application	Transport	Network	Data-Link	Physical
User/Data	Segment	Packet	Frame	Bits
1	2	3	4	5

If someone asks you the question in what order the encapsulation process belong in,
you look at the given order and use the key words to place them in the proper order

What is the correct order?

1   converts to segments

2   converts to bits

3   converts to data

4   converts to frames

5   converts to packets

Application	Transport	Network	Data-Link	Physical
User / Data	Segment	Packet	Frame	Bits
1	2	3	4	5
3	1	5	4	2

The answer is
3, 1, 5, 4, 2

Another wording for the four steps
of the data encapsulation for the TCP/IP process:

1   Transport the data (TCP/UDP)

2   Add the logical source and destination address

3   Add the MAC or local address

4   Transmit the bits after the conversion process is
    completed

Data-Encapsulation Frames

- A frame is constructed at the Data Link layer and a Trailer is appended to the data frame.

A packet is encapsulated into a frame at the Data Link layer

Encapsulation for Serial Communication

- HDLC (High Level Data Link Control) = Cisco default

- SDLC (Synchronous Data Link Control) = IBM

- LAPB (Link Access Procedure, Balanced) = X.25

Ethernet II Frame

Preamble	DA	SA	**Type**	Data	FCS
8 Bytes	6 Bytes	6 Bytes	2 Bytes	46-1500	4 Bytes

- In the DA field the first 3 bytes are vendor-dependent while the last 3 bytes are specified by IEEE 802.3.
- The DA signifies a unicast, multicast, or broadcast address
- The SA works with a unicast address under a single node
- The FCS contains the CRC

The frame is a packet transmitted across a serial line and consists of slots that can accept a value of specific attributes

The maximum transfer unit size for an ethernet frame is 1518 bytes

The 802.2 Frame

Preamble	SOP	DA	SA	**Length**	Header and Data	FCS
7 Byes	1 Byte	6 Bytes	6 Bytes	2 Bytes	46-1500 / 64 is the minimum	4 Bytes

The Header and Data field uses extra padding to reach the 64 Byte criteria

The SNAP Frame

DSAP	SSAP	Control	OUI	Ether Type	Upper Layer Data

The OUI (Organizational Unique Identifier) is the manufacturers assigned number

- DSAP is the Destination Services Access Point field that is used to provide a **memory buffer** in the receiving station.

- The DSAP contains the hexadecimal number AA. AA = two 10's.

- The DSAP and SSAP work under the Logical Link Control parameter of the Data Link Layer

The FDDI Frame

Preamble	Start Delimiter	Frame Control	DA	SA	Data	FCS	End Delimiter	Frame Status

The Token Ring Frame

Preamble	Start Delimiter	Frame Control	End Delimiter

- Token Ring uses Active Monitor to detect and compensate for errors

- Token Ring and FDDI uses the Beaconing process to self-repair itself

Data-Encapsulation Phase

The Processes of Data Movement
Sessions take place at the Transport Layer
TCP and UDP are responsible for segment delivery
Unacknowledged segments are resent
All received data is acknowledged by the sender
Segments are sequenced and put back into order upon arrival

	When using PDUs (Protocol Data Units) on a TCP/IP Ethernet network, follow these four steps for its Data-Encapsulation	
1	A TCP or UDP header is added to the data	Transport
2	**First**, the address of the destination network and the logical source are placed in the frame header. **Second**, the data is placed behind the frame header.	Network
3	The data is converted to 0s and 1s, and a header and a trailer and FCS are added to the data with the local address.	Data-Link
4	The signal is encoded and converted into bits onto the media to be transmitted.	Physical

- IP Packets are used to transmit the data between the receiving and the transmitting devices

Comparison between OSI and DOD Models

OSI Model	DOD Model	Protocols
Application	Process / Application	Telnet, FTP, LPD, SMNP, TFTP, SMTP, NFS, X-Window
Presentation		
Session		
Transport	Host-to-Host	TCP, UDP
Network	Internet	ICMP, BootP, ARP, RARP
Data-Link	Network Access	Ethernet, Fast Ethernet, Token-Ring, FDDI
Physical		

- The Host-to-Host Layer of the DOD Model is responsible for flow control with **sliding windows** and reliability with sequence numbers and acknowledgements

(Think of the Transport Layer)

Flow control is used to prevent buffer overflow at either end of the transmission

The **IP Protocol in the ICMP Protocol** is in the Internet Layer of the DOD Model. The Internet Layer is responsible for making routing decisions

The Network Access Layer maps to the Data Link and to the Physical layers of the OSI Model

File transfer Protocols at the Host-to-Host Model	
NFS (Network File System)	Uses UDP
FTP (File Transfer Protocol)	Uses TCP
TFTP (Trivial File Transfer Protocol)	Uses UDP

- TFTP file transfers usually consist of diskless workstations

- Bootstrap is used to boot diskless workstations

NOTE:

RARP and BootP
are used to boot Diskless Workstations

Passwords

- Passwords are case-sensitive

- Passwords can be set on individual interfaces

- Passwords can be set in EXEC mode *and* PRIV mode

- line vty 0 4   controls remote Telnet access to a router

- aux controls access to the auxiliary ports in the back of a router

- line con 0 controls access to the console port of the router

Console, Aux, vty are user-mode passwords

When you type   Router(config)#line vty 0 4
You get   Router(config-line)#

0 4 represents the five available virtual lines used to connect with Telnet.

The first four lines repeat themselves
whereas
the fifth vty statement should be different in case of an emergency

Passwords control access to the Priv Mode

Enter the password after the ENABLE command

The ENABLE SECRET password is encrypted and takes priority over the ENABLE password command
    Router(config)#enable secret whoISme

The auxiliary port is used to connect modems for a console or to view a dialup connection for DDR

To learn how to configure user mode passwords
    Router#config t
    Router(config)#line ?
This becomes
    Router(config-line)#

To enable the password
    Router#config t
    Router(config)#line aux 0 **or** line vty 0 4 **or** line con 0
    Router(config-line)#login
    Router(config-line)#password hello
    Router(config-line)#exit
    Router#

The Login command must be included before the password command

After you type in exit, you return to the Privilege Mode

To set a secret password
    Router(config)#enable secret [password]

To remove secret password
    Router(config)#no enable secret   *press enter*

To disable the password
    Router(config)#no password

To Telnet to another router, or computer, or mainframe
    Router#telnet [ip address]
Or
    Router#[ip address]

- You can leave the Telnet word out after the prompt

- Use Telnet to configure and check your remote router

- Telnet is a virtual terminal program that is part of the TCP/IP protocol under the Application Layer

  VTY stands for virtual terminal

  VTY must be set on the routers

- 0 4 is the five available virtual lines used to connect to Telnet

- CDP, unlike Telnet, must be directly connected to your routers

  CDP = point-to-point connection

Exec Mode

The Exec is a program in the Cisco IOS that acts as the **command interpreter** of the commands entered in the router by an operator

Exec interprets and executes

This is the user mode.
    Router>
The user mode is a subset of the Privilege mode

You can connect to remote devices in this mode

To enable:
type enable after the word router>
this becomes
    Router>enable
afterwards, this changes to
    Router#
The # sign tells you that you are now in the Privilege Mode

You can also type this command from the **User** mode
    Router>show version

To log into User Exec Mode
Press the enter key, type in your user ID, then type in your
password

To view the IOS filename. you can use the User Mode
argument
Router>show version
Or
Router>show flash

*You can achieve the same results by using the Privilege
Mode
prompt # to view the IOS filename*

The Privileged mode

- Allows you to connect to remote devices

- Allows you to modify and view the configuration of the router

- Allows you to set operating (IOS) parameters

You can run from the Privilege mode
    Router#show users,
Or
    Router#show ppp
Or
    Router#show version
Or
    Router#debug ip route
Or
    Router#debug ipx routing activity

Or to go through a series of events
    Router>   *(pres enter)*
    Router#
    Router#show interfaces
    Router#config t
    Router(config)#int e0
    Router(config-if)#ppp authentication chap
    Router(config-if)#^Z
    Router#

Router Configuration Commands

To configure the running configuration of a router (RAM)		
configure terminal	config t	commands typed by a user at the terminal
configure memory	config mem	executes commands stored in NVRAM
configure network	config net	copies a configuration file from TFTP server on the network to RAM
configure overwrite	config o	imports a configuration file directly into NVRAM, without changing any of the previous commands. This is referred to as a **gentle overlay**

configure overwrite-network
(config o)

copies a configuration file into **NVRAM** *from* a TFTP server
(this will NOT alter the running configuration)

config o = NVRAM from TFTP server

configure network
(config net)

copies the configuration file *from* a **TFTP** server
into the router's RAM

Use this when you modify or change the configuration file

130

To load a router's configuration that is stored on a tftp server into loading RAM

Router(config net)#[ip address of tftp server]

*config net = **TFTP to RAM***

NOTE

The main working network is linked to the TFTP server

configure terminal
(config t)

enters configuration commands into the router from the console port or through Telnet

The configuration file is similar to a text file in a PC

configure memory
(config mem)

executes the configuration stored in NVRAM
and
copies the router configuration file that is stored in NVRAM to RAM

NVRAM = startup-config
RAM = running-config

To add, modify, or delete, and execute the commands in the startup-config file
stored in NVRAM
And
To edit, add, or modify the startup-config file to running-config

Router#configure memory

Or

Router#config mem

This command replaces the current executing / running / active *file that is stored in NVRAM or in a configuration file on a TFTP host*

NOTE:

It is best to live with unequal distribution across multiple network paths

If configuration file is not found - the router goes to setup mode

Configuration register values determines the location of the router's operating system

0x2100, 0x2101, 0x2102

0x2142 (ignores contents of NVRAM)

To verify: Router#show version

The bootstrap loader locates the operating system image

Configuration Register

The config-register command tells the router where to get its boot system

Hexadecimal Number for Router boot up		
0x2000	RXBOOT	diagnostic usage
0x2100	To boot to Monitor Rom mode	
0x2101	To boot from ROM upgrade flash	skip NVRAM
0x2102 default	To boot from NVRAM normal operation	use NVRAM
0x2141	To boot to ROM disaster recovery	skip NVRAM
0x2142	to boot to flash password recovery	skip NVRAM

The default configuration register is 0x2102

To ensure router boots from NVRAM
 Router(config)#config-register 0x2102
Then type
 Router(config)#^Z

To view the current configuration-register settings
 Router#show version

To set up the startup dialogue
 Router#setup

The initial configuration dialogue starts when

1 It is the first time the router has been powered on

2 The write erase command was executed immediately before powering down the router

Password Recovery

Password recovery uses 0x2142

This ignores NVRAM during startup

To ignore NVRAM so you can start the router without the password

    Router(config)#config-register 0x2142
    Router(config)#^Z

Then start over with the new password

    Router#config t
    Router(config)#line aux 0   **or**   line vty 0 4
or   line con 0
    Router(config-line)#login
    Router(config-line)#password newME

To change the enable secret password itISme

    Router(config)# enable secret itISme

- Passwords are case sensitive.

IOS Movement Commands

Ctrl + Shift + x
   telnets into multiple routers and keep all sessions open at the same time as you work from the console of the main router

Ctrl + shift key + 6
   takes you to another router that you want to work with
(If you add an x instead of a 6 it will take you back to the main router)

Ctrl + Z   same as   ^ + Z or ^Z
   Ends configuration mode and **returns** to the Privilege Exec mode   *Router#*

Ctrl + A
   Moves the cursor to the beginning of the current line
   ie: Router(config)#| ←...................

TAB
   Lets you finish typing a command
   Router# run ....→|..........

Ctrl + C
   Returns you to Privilege Exec prompt (#) without making changes or without running through the entire system configuration dialogue

Ctrl + ^
   Cancels copy from flash memory

How can you return from the interface configuration mode back to the global configuration mode?

Type in the Exit command and it will take you back one level

Remember: Ctrl + Z as well as Ctrl + C will return you to the root level

Router#int e1
Router(config-if)#**exit**
Router(config)#

Ctrl + P or the ↑ keyboard up arrow
     Recalls previous command and lets you view the **router's history** up to 10 lines

Ctrl + N or the ↓ keyboard down arrow moves the cursor to the **most recent** command after you have used the Ctrl + P command.

→ Keyboard right arrow moves the cursor one character to the right

← Keyboard left arrow moves the cursor one character to the left

Current Active Mode Commands

Router>	User mode
Router#	Privilege mode
Router(config)#	Global mode
Router(config-if)#	Interface mode
Router(config-line)#	password
Router(config-hub)#	device argument mode
Router(config-map-class)#	maps to class configuration
Router(config-route-map)#	maps the route configuration
Router(config-router)#	after RIP or IGRP is set up
Router(config-**ipx**-router)#	after IPX is set up
Router(config-router-map)#	after the map command in Frame Relay is set up
Router(config-controller)#	after the ISDN T1 and E1 lines are set up
Router(config-subif)#	after the subinterface is set

*A Router's **subset** does not enter into any mode configuration*

138

IOS User Mode Commands

To get to User Exec Mode from the console, press the enter key

To get back to the User Mode type
Or
To go from PRIV Mode to USER Mode
     Router#disable
Or
     Router#logout

*This CLI is not the same as Router(**config**)#logout*

This commands takes you to
     Router>
This is the User Mode

If you type
     Router>enable
Or
     Router>en
This takes you to
     Router#

To make global changes
     Router#config terminal
Or
     Router#config t

When you type
   Router#config t   *(same as configuration terminal)*
This will put you in
   Router(config)#

This puts you in global configuration mode and into the running-config area

Runs in Dynamic RAM

When you type to logout of the router
   Router(config)#exit
Or
   Router(config)#logout
this takes you back to
   Router(config)#

This is the global command
whereas
the other logout argument is rendered in the subcommand

Watch for the difference in Router#logout

IOS Boot System Commands

A router usually boots from the commands in the startup configuration file

Boot commands are based on hardware platform

Last resort boot and to boot router from the IOS in RAM
Router(config)#boot system rom

To have the router boot from the specified IOS image
Or
To boot from the first image in flash, if no image is specified, type
Router(config)#boot system flash

If you need to boot the router by loading the IOS from a remote tftp server,
Or
To have the router load IOS from a tftp server
Router(config)#boot system tftp [file name] [ip address of tftp server]

This boot up method will prevent a major outage if your current IOS becomes corrupt

To **save** changes or to make a new copy to NVRAM
Router#copy running-config startup-config
Or
Router#copy run start

To **store** an extra copy of the router's startup configuration
on a remote TFTP server
for backup purposes
    Router#copy startup-config tftp

To rerun the initial System Configuration dialog
Or
To reconfigure your Cisco router after a corrupt file
Or
When you want to upgrade your router's IOS
    Router#setup

NOTE:
Don't forget that RXboot is used to load the image file to
flash

RXboot works in the Router's subset command area

IOS NVRAM & RAM Commands

If NVRAM is erased and a new IOS is reloaded,
the router will start in setup mode

This initial file will load into the working storage area of NVRAM. Or, in other words, this first file copy will be stored in NVRAM's backup memory. This is the only time NVRAM will store an original configuration start-up file.

To restore a configuration file to RAM
    Router#copy tftp running-config

This copies from a tftp server to the router.

The **copy running-config tftp** command
copies the running configuration   to   a TFTP server
not from one.

It does not copy the tftp configuration

It does not copy the startup config file

To copy a configuration file from a TFTP server to the startup configuration in NVRAM

    Router#copy tftp startup-config

To display a running-config file to a console terminal
Or
To see **multiple changes** to the running variables on the router
Or
To review the contents of RAM

    Router#show running-config

In RAM this file can be erased

show running-config is used by RAM. It is the active configuration file

show startup-config is used by NVRAM

NVRAM is the backup configuration file for the running configuration file

To copy the **currently executing** configuration file to NVRAM

    Router#copy running-config startup-config

The startup configuration file that exists in NVRAM will be overwritten

> NVRAM contains the backup configuration files
>
> RAM contains the active configuration files

Flash contains the IOS. If no image is in flash, the router will go to ROM

You must use the **Route Table** to find information about destination networks

The route table also contains the metric table information

Three methods to review the contents of RAM

    Router#show protocols

Or

    Router#show version

Or

    Router#show running-config

The Router#show version will also display the boot images, the names and sources of the configuration files and the software version of the IOS

The show running-config displays the running configuration file to a console terminal

Two methods to review the contents of NVRAM
    Router#show configuration
Or
    Router#show startup-config

To delete the startup-config file
    Router#erase startup-config

IOS TFTP Commands

To copy new variables that you have configured to a tftp
server
    Router#copy flash tftp

To backup IOS software
Or
To backup a router
    Router#copy flash tftp

To copy the old image to a tftp server
Or
To copy the contents of flash to a tftp host
    Router#copy flash tftp

To backup the IOS to the load device using tftp
    Router#copy flash tftp

The IOS is stored in flash by default and uses UDP packets

To restore IOS to a router
Or
To upgrade the IOS from a remote server
Or
To copy a new version into flash memory
Or
To start an IOS file image upgrade
    Router#copy tftp flash

The new IOS must reside on the tftp server

copy tftp flash tells the router to copy the contents of TFTP to flash memory

To display the total router memory, the remaining available memory, and the name of the system image file
    Router#show flash

To have the router boot from the file Molly on a tftp sever on an ip address, type in
    Router(config)#boot system tftp Molly [ip address]

IOS Start, Run, & Logging Commands

To reload the router
    Router#reload

To **save** the file from RAM to NVRAM
    Router#copy running-config startup-config
Or
    Router#copy run start

To see the router's **current** configuration
    Router#sh run

To see the backup configuration stored in NVRAM
    Router#sh start

To reduce the strain on the router's CPU
And
To configure the router to create logs, use
    syslog server routing

IOS Banner & Description Commands

To add a banner
Or
To enable a banner
    Router(config)#banner motd #....#   *(or !.....! or*
&......&)

The login is displayed after the motd banner,
followed by the password,
then finally the EXEC banner

A banner adds security notice to users

The #, ! and &, in this usage, are called delimiters.
Any symbol can act as a delimiter: $, !, %, etc.

The motd is displayed at login

To type in a description text
    Router(config-**if**)#description [text]

The descriptive text is rendered with the interface command

IOS Hostname Commands

To establish a hostname for your router
Router(config)#hostname Jacksonville
This becomes
Jacksonville(config)#

The hostname is locally significant.
*The keyword here is **establish**.*

The hostname cannot be over 63 characters long

To resolve, create or **assign** a host name to a router
Or
To type Jacksonville instead of the ip address to access the router
Router(config)#ip host Jacksonville 123.45.67.1
Or
Router(config)ip host [hostname] [ip address]

*This CLI uses **ip** in its statement and has the **ip address** statement*

You can configure up to 8 address

To discover **ALL** the host names and their **corresponding** IP address, and the flags, and protocol types in your router, type:
Router#show hosts
Or
Router#show hostnames

This one also lets you see the configured host names on your router

To remove the host name
Router(config)#no ip host Jacksonville

To view the configured hosts names
Router#sh host

To change the names of your Router that you are working on
Router#config t
Router(config)#hostname router Jacksonville
Jacksonville(config)#^+Z
Jacksonville#

Then start again with your CLI

To disable
Or
To turn off DNS lookup
Router#no ip domain-lookup

To enable your router to search *(look)* for a domain
Router(config)#ip name-server [ip address]

You can enable two DNS severs to query

Don't forget: 6 ip addresses are the maximum for the DNS

DNS = name to IP resolution

NOTE:

An ip host can define a static host name
(ip host Jacksonville [ip address])

IOS ISDN Commands

To find out whether a specific interface was configured as DCE or DTE

> Router#show controllers serial

Or

> Router#show controller

Or

> Router#show controllers serial1

Three methods to monitor ISDN or DDR

> Router#show interface

Or

> Router#show controllers

Or

> Router#show dialers

To view the device IP, the hardware platform, the software version, the port type, all the numbers of local and remote neighbors, and the holdtime, type in:

> Router#show cdp neighbors detail

To rerun the initial System Configuration dialog so you can reconfigure your router

> Router#setup

To see the status

> Router#show isdn status

IOS Interface Commands

To view access lists
Or
To see real-time statistics
Or
To monitor frame-relay
    Router#show interface

To display information on each router's interface
and
To identify which interfaces have an access list
    Router#show ip interface
Or
    Router#show running-config

You can only enter one configuration change, one per line.
End with ctrl+Z   (^+Z)

Type **Router#copy run start** *to save your changes*

To show MTU size
Router#show ip interface

The Local Area Networks using Ethernet

Size is determined by the network hardware

MTU uses serial lines

For long haul communication MTU uses software to determine size

To see the configuration information of your serial port 1
Router#show interface s1

When you type
Router(config)#interface e0   or   int e0   or
Ethernet 0,
and press enter, it places you in
Router(config-if)#

To make changes to an interface
Router(config)#interface ?

If you want to verify your configuration after you have forgotten which interface you were on, use this command:

    Router#sh int ?

The ? will display to you the router's interfaces)

To verify the known interface

    Router#sh int e0

To display the configuration information of all the interfaces

    Router#show interface

Or

    Router#sh int e0

Or

    Router#sh int s0

These three command lines will display the hardware address,
the logical address, the encapsulation method,
and the statistics on the number of collisions

IOS IPX Commands

What does the ipx maximum paths command do?
It forwards the IPX packets over multiple paths to improve load sharing

Up to 6 paths

To display the ipx routing updates **in or out** between routers
Or
To monitor IPX traffic
    Router#show ipx traffic

To see if your router is receiving SAP and RIP information on an interface, type in:
    Router#sh ipx int

To see if the router is hearing the SAP's in your server
    Router#sh ipx servers

To see the IPX address and encapsulation type
    Router#sh protocols

To see the interface status of IPX
    Router#sh **ipx** int e0

Do not confuse with Router#sh int e0 *as this one displays the IP address*

To show updates, and the source and the destination addresses for IPX
    Router#debug ipx routing activity

To see which interfaces have IP access groups set on them
    Router#show ip interface

If you type
    Router(config-if)#exit *(These are rendered in the interface)*
Or
    Router(config-if)#logout
It takes you back to
    Router(config)#...(This is global)

To manually override a default tick metric in an IPX interface
    Router#ipx delay [number]

(WAN = 6,   LAN = 1)

IOS IP Route Static Commands

Routers learn destination paths by:

    1   Static
    2   Default
    3   Dynamic routing

- A static route defines a path to an IP destination network

- A static route builds routing tables to a remote network.

- A static route creates a static route only when you have a few routers and to save bandwidth

To create an IP static route
    Router(config)#ip route [destination_network_address] [subnet_mask]
[next_hop_address or default gateway]
[administrative_distance] [permanent]

This is the same as

Router(config)#ip route [ip address] 255.255.255.0 [ip address]

A gateway is required. The Administrative_Distance is optional

The gateway parameter is used to determine the next hop

To configure a given IP address along with its mask
     Router(config-**if**)# [ip address] [mask]
(interface command)

To set a gateway of last resort
     Router(config)#ip route 0.0.0.0 0.0.0.0 [default gateway]   *(global command)*
Or
     Router(config)#ip classless

To remove default routes configured on the router
     Router(config)#no ip route 0.0.0.0 0.0.0.0 123.45.6.1
     Router(config)#no shut

     *Do a **no shut** after entering an IP addresses*

To set up a default gateway
     Router(config)#ip default-gateway [ip address]

To create a default IP route to send ALL packets received to a specific router
     Router(config)#ip route 0.0.0.0 0.0.0.0 111.12.34.1

To create a gateway of last resort
     Router(config)#ip route 0.0.0.0 0.0.0.0 [gateway ip address]

To remove default routes configured on the IP routing table
    Router(config)#no ip route 0.0.0.0 0.0.0.0 [ip address]
Or
    Router(config)#clear ip route [network | mask]

To clear everything from the routing table use the * asterisk
    Router#clear ip route *

To verify the static route
    Router#sh ip route
Or
    Router#ping [ip address]

To create a static route to see another network address
    Router(config)#ip route 123.45.10.0 255.255.255.0
123.45.73.1
Translated
    Router(config)#ip route [network] [mask] [address | interface] [Admin Distance]

The first group of numbers after the ip route comprise the
destination *ip address,*
followed by the subnet mask, then followed by the **source**
ip address

Destination first!   **Source second!**

Static routes must be manually established and manually
updated

To remove static routes from the Router
   Router(config)#no ip route 123.45.17.1 255.255.255.0
123.45.68.1

To create a default route for an IP network that will not use
EIGRP or OSPF
   Router(config)#ip route 0.0.0.0 0.0.0.0 [next-hop]

A Static IP Address Scenario

Your newly promoted boss wants you to help him identify the IP address and the wildcard mask that will match hosts 68-104.

He gives you a piece a paper that has written on it: use the IP address 223.123.245.67. It also gives you the subnet mask, 255.2255.255.240

First: we read the wadded paper after straightening it out. We discern that the IP address and the subnet mask compose the 6 high order bits in the 4th octet and that leaves us the lower two bits to work with to discover the host addresses.

128	64	32	16	8	4	2	1
1	1	1	1	0	1	0	0
240 = these 6 high order bits are used for the subnetting						These 2 low order bits are used for the hosts addresses	

Second: we need to match the host of 24-46. This will require two sets of IP address and two sets of wildcard masks. Why two sets? Because we need to discern each entity.

Third: we begin with the first parameter, the IP address of 223.123.245.67. We subtract from the 4th octet 67 from 104 which will result in 37, and from this we must subtract another one, which will present to us the wildcard of 0.0.0.36. This permits us to match the host 67 – 103.

Fourth: The answer becomes:

    223.123.245.67 0.0.0.36 223.123.245.104 0.0.0.0 to match the specified host range.

Wow, dig this, the kid really, really likes you. Your promotion is right around the corner.

Another play at the office:

The same boss now gives you the IP address 183.123.245.0 255.255.255.0 and now he wants you to identify the wildcard mask that will match the subnets 183.123.245.0 – 183.123.254.0 and all the hosts on the subnets

Subtract 245 from 254 to get 9. Mask out the remaining bits in both octets

The wildcard mask is 0.0.9.255

IOS List and ? Commands

When you type the control key ^ and Z at the same time on the keyboard
    Router(config)#^ + Z
It takes you to
    Router#

> *This action takes you out of the configuration mode*
> *and places you back at the **Privilege Mode***

> *The carrot ^ is over the number 6 on the keyboard*

To see the **list** of commands
    Router#?

To find commands that starts with a specific letter
    Router#r?
this discovers run rant rage as the r is filled in with the remaining letters r.....

To find the **next** command **in a string** and to find out what they do

    Router#run **?**

this discovers running, runts and explains what they do

A space is required after the word and before the ?

If you forget the command and the % Ambiguous command
"clc"
shows up on the screen, correct by retyping the ?

NOTE:

The operating system works upon the statements
in the configuration file which holds the access-lists file

IOS Debug Commands

To enable all possible debugging
    Router#debug all

Problem: the debug command severely impacts the router's performance

To turn off all debugging activity
    Router#undebug all
Or
    Router#no debug all

To view all the debugging activity that is currently enabled
    Router#show debug

IOS RIP & IGRP Commands

To configure and enable RIP
    Router#config t
    Router(config)#router rip
    Router(config-router)#network [ip address]
    Router(config-router)#^Z
    Router#

To configure IGRP
    Router#config t
    Router(config)#router igrp [autonomous system number request]
    Router(config-router)#network [ip address]
    Router(config-router)#^Z
    Router#

When you type
    Router(config)#router igrp
*you get an **Autonomous system** number request.*

Don't forget the ip address parameter is required

The AS is a group of networks under the control of a single administrator. Only the routers with the same AS number can communicate with each other. The lower the AS number, the more trusting it is.

To verify that **RIP** is running on your router
    Router#show ip protocol
Or
    Router #show ip route
Or
    Router#show running-config
Or
    Router#show run
Then press the enter key

When you type router rip *to enable it*
    Router(config)#router rip
This becomes
    Router(config-router)#

NOTE:

After you have enabled RIP,
you can enable the network simply by adding the command
after the statement

IOS Clock Rate Commands

To set clock rate
    Router(config-if)#clock rate 125,000   *(interface command)*

To set the bandwidth
    Router(config-if)#bandwidth 64   *(no zeros)*

The clock rate is set in bits

The bandwidth rate is set in kilobits

*The clock rate provides clocking simulation
on a serial DTE/DCE interface*

To display the current time
    Router#show clock

To display the clock rate configured on the serial interface
    Router#sh running-config
Or
    Router#sh controllers s0

To view files
    Router#sh run

IOS History Commands

To display the last 10 commands you typed
Router#sh history

10 is the default size

To increase the history size
Router#terminal history size [#]
Then type
Router#sh history

256 is the maximum

To enable history
Or
To enable the editing feature
Router#terminal editing

To disable history
Or
To **turn off** the **advance editing** features
Router#terminal no editing

To verify broadcast frequency
    Router#sh ip protocol

To establish an Administrative Distance
    Router(config)#distance weight [address mask]
[access-list-number | name] [ip]

*The weight is the default admin distance number from 10-
255*

IOS IP Address Commands

To add an IP address
    Router(config)#123.111.78.0 255.255.0.0
    Router(config)#no shutdown
same as
    Router(config)#[ip address] [mask]

     Must do a no shutdown to enable the interface

    You can configure the router's ip address from the
       terminal, memory, or network areas

All the steps of configuration
    Router>
    Router>enable
    Router#config t
    Router(config)#hostname Molly
    Molly(config)#interface e0
    Molly(config-if)#ip address 123.45.67.1 255.255.255.0
    Molly(config-if)#no shutdown

  The IP address argument is followed by the numeric IP
          address,
    which is followed by the mask argument

To view the IP routing tables
    Router#sh ip route

IOS CDP & MAC & Initial System Commands

To view the cdp packets
and
To see if the CDP is enabled
    Router#show cdp

Cisco Discovery Protocol gathers information about neighboring Cisco devices
to verify their connectivity and to discover the neighboring router's network address

To view ALL the router's information on the CDP neighbors
    Router#show cdp neighbor details
Or
    Router#sh cdp entry *   *(requires an asterisk)*

To disable CDP on all interfaces
    Router(config-if)#no cdp run

To see the MAC address
    Router#show mac-address-table   *(Use 2 hyphens)*

To either increase or decrease the values of the cdp timer
    Router(config)#cdp timer 60
Or
    Router(config)#cdp holdtime 120

This changes the cdp timer. 60 seconds is the default

Problem IOS Commands

Router#copy tftp startup-config

Copies a configuration file from a tftp server
to the startup configuration in NVRAM

Router#copy startup-config tftp

Copies the startup configuration file in NVRAM
to a **remote** TFTP server

Use this command to store an extra copy of the router's startup configuration on a remote server for backup purposes

---

Router#show startup-config

displays the startup configuration of the router
and
it displays the backup configuration file

NVRAM = startup-config

RAM = running-config

NOTE:
This command is not the same as
Router#copy startup-config

175

Router#show ip protocol

is used to see the routing protocols in use for IP on the entire router,
as well as the **update frequency**,
and **filter** information, current **timer** values,
and to verify **broadcast** frequency

Router#show ip route

is used to display the contents of the routing tables
and
will display all known routes on the router

It will also display the gateway address,
the router interface used,
the number of seconds since an advertisement was received for the route,
and the administrative and metric values.

The administrative and metric are shown in brackets [admin # / metric #]
to flag the new routers discovered by IGRP

A metric is a calculated value that is measured in ticks and hops

Router#show running-config

This command will display the **active** configuration parameters, and the configured clock rate on the serial interface

Not the same as Router#running-config

Router#erase startup-config

erases the startup configuration file from NVRAM

Router#copy running-config startup-config

Or

Router#copy run start

copies the running configuration **from** RAM to the
startup configuration file in NVRAM

or

to **save** changes to your running configuration to the configuration file
that is stored in NVRAM

In pre 10.3 version, use the write memory or write argument

RAM = running-config

NVRAM = startup-config

Router#copy startup-config running-config

Or

Router#copy start run

copies the startup configuration to the running configuration in RAM

This command is also **used to restore** and return the router
to its original configuration status

To do this, you must not have committed the changes that you have made

configure overwrite-network
(config o)

copies a configuration file into NVRAM **from** a TFTP server

formula:

Use reverse thinking

From tftp to NVRAM

---

configure network
(config net)

copies the configuration file **from** a TFTP server
into the router's RAM

tftp = network

---

configure terminal
(config t)

is used to enter configuration commands into the router
from the console port reviewed through Telnet

---

configure memory

executes the configuration stored in NVRAM

To create a static / default route
that will send **all** packets received to router's ip address

Router(config)#ip route 0.0.0.0 0.0.0.0 [ip address]

Router#debug ip rip

displays **RIP** routing updates sent and received through **IP**

(Do not confuse with IPX)

Router#debug ipx routing activity

displays **IPX** routing update packets sent and received
and
displays the source and destination addresses in IPX

copy running-config tftp
copies the running configuration (RAM) to a tftp file from a network server or from a remote file

copy run start
is the same as write memory

copy run tftp
is the same as write network

Router#show interface

This one is my personal enemy. We first met in the jungles of terror, where I went through a mad frenzy shouting all night long: "Show your interface!"

This command will display each and every statistic out there!

The configurations on the switch, the switch trunk,
the switch line ports (yes!), shows output queue
along with their hardware and their potential conflicts.

The IP and IPX address
but you must specify which in the command line
(Router#sh int e0 = IP)
Router#sh ipx int e0 **or** *sh ipx int = IPX*

The changes in the serial (s0, s1) and in the ethernet (e0, e1) ports

The statistics on the routers and their network interfaces,
the router's output and keepalives

And, it displays the DLCI and **line speed** of the Frame Relay network

It displays the ARP stuff, as well as the **SAP and RIP updates**

It displays the packets, the runts, and the giants.

And, it is also **used to verify** duplex settings on the interface.

Most Important: it is also **used to verify** and **monitor** Access Lists

---

Router#sh ip interface brief
reveals the
summary of all interfaces and their IP addresses

status = interface

Router#show version

This one is a problem because it does so much.

It displays

the names and sources of the configuration files,

the software version of the IOS,

the configuration-register values,

the hardware platform,

and the boot images.

However,

it does not verify nor monitor!

IOS Commands Help Guide

To copy a new version of the IOS image from a network
sever into flash
Or
To load a new IOS image into your router from tftp

copy tftp flash

This translates to		
copy	network server	flash
load	router	
copy	**tftp**	**flash**

Formula

copy	**from**	**to**

You have just made a change to (updated) your router
running configuration
and you want to save this to the configuration that is stored
in NVRAM

copy running-config startup-config

This translates to		
save	copies from the running configuration in RAM	copies to the startup configuration file in NVRAM
copy	**running-config**	**startup-config**

Formula

copy	**from**	**to**

After modifying the running configuration (RAM) on your router you realize you configured the wrong router. You now want to remove the new settings on the router before they are fully committed to the router. In order to return to the original configuration settings on the router that you made the changes to, you must use the following command:

copy startup-config running-config

This translates to		
restore/ recopy	the startup configuration file in NVRAM	to the original running configuration file in RAM
copy	startup-config	running-config
same as		
copy	**start**	**run**

It is an interesting thing that whenever a new configuration file is created in WordPad or another text program and when the new stuff is copied into RAM, the new configuration will merge with the previously existing configuration. It does not destroy it, but intertwines gently with what once was. The cute term for this is: "**gentle overlay**".

Transmission Control Protocol

- TCP is a Layer 4 function - Transport Layer Protocol

- TCP provides sequencing, acknowledgements, and the creation of virtual circuits.

- TCP is responsible for delivery of packets and datagrams and frames in their order to identify and place the packet in their correct order.

  *This is referred to as TCP's **reliability** factor*

- TCP successfully delivers packets through acknowledgements, windowing, and flow control, performed through a process similar to a three-way handshake

- TCP begins it three-way handshake process when

  1 The originating source sends an **Initial Sequence Number** to a destination.

  2 The destination, when it receives the packet, acknowledges it and in return, sends its own INS signal to the originating source,

  3 which then proceeds to acknowledge it

TCP defines hosts as one for each router interface, and one for each NIC card on each computer or printer. Eleven PC's plus one laser printer equals 12 hosts. In a Class C address scheme this translates to subnet mask 255.255.255.240

User Datagram Protocol

- UDP is a Transport Layer Protocol – layer 4

- UDP makes a best effort delivery that is not guaranteed

- UDP is not reliable

- UDP is a connectionless protocol

  !!!!!!!!!!!!!!!!!! indicates that one UDP frame has successfully transmitted

- UDP uses **ports**

- UDP does not use windowing or acknowledgements

- UDP does not use the three way handshake for transmitting data

- UDP **relies** on the upper layers to provide reliability for its transmitted packets

NOTE:

UDP is used by NFS, SNMP, DNS, and TFTP

187

Internet Protocol

- The network, the subnet, and the host are the three paths of an ip address

- IP is a connectionless, best-effort packet dialing services. IP is similar to UDP

- The IP Datagram has a source address and a destination address that transports data

- IP packets and datagrams are exchanged between the network layers of the transmitting and receiving devices that works with LAN and WAN

A Data-Link Switch is used to transport IBM System's Network Architecture & NetBIOS traffic over an IP Network

- IP provides no error checking and it is not reliable. IP depends on TCP for error checking

- IP does NOT check the data field. IP only checks the header field

- Each Layer 3 device in the network requires its own IP address **interface** A router, the Proxy server and a firewall require a logical network address as it helps establish each individual identity of the device to the management.

- Each Layer 1 and 2 devices in the network requires its own IP address. The Hub and the Switch do not address their ports individually. The Network-layer address may be required by the managers. If not, then skip it.

To configure an IP address in decimal
    Router(config)#int e0
    Router(config-if)#ip address 131.3.4.5 255.255.255.0
    Router(config-if)#no shutdown

A no shutdown command turns on an interface

To add a second IP address in decimal
    Router(config-if)#ip address 131.3.4.5 255.255.255.0
secondary

To verify an ip address
    Router#sh run

- IP makes routing decisions at the Internet layer of the DOD model

- The IP address can also be rendered in binary and hexadecimal

- IP can also work with a single host name on two separate IP addresses.

To commit 2 hostnames to 1 IP address
    Router(config-if)#ip hostname [tcp port #] address [address]
Or
    IP host P1R1 [ip address] [ip address]

You must have two ip address statements
when you use the P1R1 structure

The Loopback Address is 127.0.0.1

189

The three **Private** network addresses are: 10.0.0.0-255, 172.16.0.0 - 176.31.0255, and 192.168.0.0-255

To monitor IP
Router#show ip interface
Or
Router#show ip protocol
Or
Router#show ip route

To set the IP network for a specific numerical usage line
Router(config-if)term ip network [bitcount | decimal | hexadecimal]

An IP network is set on the Session Layer level when you use the Privilege Exec Mode

Hexadecimal numbers: A = 10, B = 11, C = 12, D = 13, E = 14, F = 15

Thus 0F + A = 25. A − 0D = 3

NOTE:

IP = logical network addressing

Internet Control Message Protocol

- ICMP is an IP Protocol

- ICMP reports IP errors and handles control messages

- Routers and hosts use ICMP to send reports of problems about datagrams back to the original source that sent the datagram

- ICMP uses PING and Trace route. *(Associated with Destination Unreachable)*

You can block a ping at the router by using an access lists

deny icmp any any echo-request

Or

deny icmp any any eq 8

- ICMP sends **redirects** back to the originating router if the destination device is unreachable and if that device is congested.

- If congested, the device drops the packets

ICMP type numbers	
8	is for echo
0	is for echo reply
30	is for trace route
37	is for domain name request

1 ICMP uses **echo request / response** function to determine if the destination is reachable and is responding

2 ICMP's **Time exceeded** valve can detect circular packets

3 The **Information Request / Reply** gets a network's address

4 The **Timestamp / Reply** estimates the transit time that a packets remains in the network

5 The **Destination Unreachable** message that reports the unreachable destination is the most common error message

These are the four additional subcategories

network unreachable
host unreachable
protocol unreachable
port unreachable

6 The **Source Quench** reports on the flow control

Address Resolution Protocol

- ARP is in the OSI **Network** Layer

- ARP is a Distance-Vector Protocol

ARP maps an IP address to a MAC address

ARP stores this new, learned, information in the ARP cache

To view the information in ARP
    Router#show arp

- ARP is a dynamic part of the TCP/IP protocol, which makes ARP a **dynamic** protocol

- ARP works across a single physical network and is limited in the amount of discovery hops that it can make: 15 is its maximum distance.

- ARP can bind an IP address to a physical hardware of a NIC card. (This is referred to the **BIA**. *(The vendor provides the Burned-In-Address)*

Reverse Address Resolution Protocol

- The RARP is used to resolve a MAC address to an IP address

Or, in other words

- The RARP is used to get an IP address from a known MAC address

BootP will also permit hosts to do the same thing

NOTE:

Use this formula:
when it is from a known [IP / MAC] use reverse thinking

from *this* to *that*

Internetwork Packet Exchange

- IPX is a Layer 3 (Network Layer) NetWare Protocol that also happens to be Novell's proprietary connectionless protocol. IPX uses Remote Procedure Calls (RPC) to communicate with the remote server. As IPX is a connectionless protocol, it is similar to IP's parameters.

- IPX uses its own class of RIP that is similar to IP's RIP. Both are dynamic distance vector-routing protocols, however IPX RIP sends out their updates every 60 seconds, whereas IP's RIP sends out their updates every 30 seconds.

- IPX also incorporates the usage of a "tick" as its metric, and allocates the policy that if two paths have an identical "tick", the chosen path will be based on it "hop count" rather than the "tick" measurement. IPX's RIP uses hexadecimal address scheme whereas IP's RIP uses decimal addressing schemes.

- IPX uses a 32 bit long network number and a 48 bit long node number (MAC), for a total of 80 bits. Because IPX uses the vendor's MAC number that is burned into the EEPROM of the NIC card, it is fairly simple for the NOS to find its host. IP's RIP has to use ARP to discover its destination address.

IPX uses 10 bytes in its address scheme.
It is the Administrator who is responsible for creating the network's addressing formula,
the network values, the network nodes, and the server parameters

- IPX also uses NFS, TFTP, PPP and SNMP

IPX works at Layer 3 of the OSI model – the Network Layer

- SPX is Novell's proprietary reliable, connection-oriented protocol

SPX works at Layer 4 of the OSI model – the Transport Layer

- NLSP (NetWare Link Services Protocol) is Novell's proprietary link-state protocol

*NLSP supports 127 hops, load balancing across parallel paths, checks for connectivity in the links through the use of **adjacency** criteria*

- NCP (NetWare Core Protocol) provides client-to-server connections

IPX can use UDP to support TCP/IP Suite. IPX encapsulates their datagrams inside UDP/IP headers for transport across the IP internetwork

IPX must be enabled through the router's CLI

To enable IPX   *(IP is enabled by default)*
    Router#config t
    Router((config)#ipx routing
    Router(config)#ctrl + Z   (^ + Z)
    Router#

To enable IPX on individual interfaces   *(int e0   int to0   int s0)*
    Router#config t
    Router(config)# ipx routing
    Router(config)#int e0   *(this command line will present an **if** on the next line)*
    Router(config-if)#ipx network [#]
    Router(config-if)#^Z
    Router#

***if** stands for interface*

Put a number value at [#]

NOTE:

The metric counts:

WAN = 6   LAN = 1

To override the metric defaults, use
    Router(config-if)#ipx delay

To see the IPX metric values
    Router#show ipx route
Or
    Router#show ipx server

198

To test your IPX configuration
    Router#sh ipx route

C	Connected Directly
S	Statically connected
R	RIP
E	EIGRP

One parallel is path allowed

15 hops are allowed. The 16th makes it unreachable

To see a router's IPX address configuration
    Router#sh ipx int
Or
    Router#sh int

Three methods to monitor your IPX access lists
    Router#sh access-lists
Or
    Router#sh ipx int
Or
    Router#sh interface

To display the IPX address configured on interface e0
    Router#sh ipx int
Or
    Router#sh ipx int e0
Or
    Router#sh ipx ethernet0

To see the IPX address and encapsulation type
  Router#sh protocols

To see the interface status of IPX
  Router#sh ipx int e0

> *Do not confuse with* Router#sh int e0 *as this one displays the IP address*

To see routing update packets
Or
To display routing **update** packets transmitted and received between routers
Or
To show both the source and destination addresses in IPX
  Router#debug ipx routing activity
same as
  Router#debug ipx routing [events | activity]

To turn off routing updates
  Router#undebug ipx routing activity

IPX Service Advertisement Protocol

IPX uses SAP (Service Advertisement Protocol) to announce their file servers, print servers, and to advertise their network addresses. This information is updated every 60 seconds.

(Router Access Lists can filter SAP broadcasts)

T reduce SAP broadcasts use: EIGRP, NLSP, and SAP filters on the Access Lists

To see SAP activity
Router#debug ipx sap activity

To see the servers discovered through SAP
Router#show ipx servers

To permit all IPX SAPs
Router(config)#access-list permit –1

The order in which to create a SAP access List:

SAP source, SAP type, SAP name

NOTE:

From NetWare 4.0 plus, SAP's usage has been reduced in favor of
NDS (NetWare Directory Services) Server.

SAP is still used by the network's workstations when they need to locate the NDS Server

IPX Maximum Paths

What does the ipx maximum paths command do?
It forwards IPX packets over multiple paths to improve
load sharing.
Also, it can configure round-robin sharing over multiple
equal metric paths.
It can do this up to 6 paths.

To perform a **round-robin** load balance over multiple
equal-cost paths
Or
To forward IPX packets over multiple paths to improve
load sharing
   Router(config)#ipx maximum-paths [#]

Goes from number 1 to 512

To configure multiple frame types
Or
To add a second network address with IPX

First:

   Router#config t
   Router(config)#int **e0**
   Router(config-if)#ipx network 10a encapsulation [arpa | novell-
ether | sap | hdlc | snap | novell-fddi] sec

Second:

   Router(config)#int e0.1
   Router(config-if)#ipx network 10a encapsulation arpa secondary
   Router(config-if)#^Z   *(ctrl + Z)*
   Router#

To see the IPX address of an interface
    Router#sh protocol
Or
    Router#sh ipx interface

To permit both Ethernet_802.2 and Ethernet_802.3 frame types to coexist on the same network when you have a new NetWare 4.11 server along with several older NetWare 3.11 servers.
    Router#config t
    Router(config)#int e0
    Router(config-if)#ipx network 123 encap sap sec
    Router(config-if)#ctrl + Z
    Router#
Or
    Router(config)#int e0.112
    Router(config-if)#ipx network 123 encap sap

The period before 123 indicates a subinterface

The preferred way of adding a secondary address to an interface
is to configure a subinterface

Whenever you add a new 4.11 NetWare server to an existing network that is utilizing NetWare 3.11 servers and you wish to configure the new 4.11 servers to use NetWare's default frame type, all you have to do is add the SAP encapsulation to the command line. By doing this, it permits **multiple** frame types to communicate on a **single wire** even though each network has a different number assigned to it.

Don't forget, use SNAP in the case of TCP and AppleTalk,
use arpa in the case of Ethernet_II,
use sap with Token_Ring

To create a subinterface
    Router(config)#interface e0.111
Or
    Router(config)#int s0/0.1
The new CLI is
    Router(config-**subif**)#

The period **.** *in the statement is crucial to have*

Subinterfaces create virtual interfaces within the router

int s0.xx {multipoint / point-to-point}

Problem IPX commands

To see IPX packets received and transmitted

Or

To view the statistics

Or

To display the IPX routing updates in or out between routers

Router#sh ipx traffic

To view the number of broadcasts that your router is receiving

Or

To view the SAP broadcasts

Or

To view the SAP table

Router#show ipx server

To view the messages that describe each SAP update

Router#debug ipx sap [event | activity]

Default IPX FRAME Types

Netware's Terminology	Cisco's Terminology
Ethernet_802.3	Novell-ether (also called raw ether) *default for NetWare version 2 – 3.11*
Ethernet_802.2	SAP *post NetWare 3.12 +*
Ethernet_II	ARPA *supports TCP/IP, DECnet, and IPX*
Ethernet_SNAP	SNAP *supports TCP/IP, IPX, and AppleTalk*
Token Ring	SAP *default*
Token Ring_SNAP	SNAP
FDDI_SNAP	SNAP *default*
FDDI_802.2	SAP
FDDI_Raw	Novell-fddi
serial synchronous links	HDLC

Thus, the default encapsulation on a **serial router interface** is hdlc

IPX Encapsulation

- SAP indicates Ethernet 802.2, Token Ring, FDDI SAP

- SNAP indicates Ethernet SNAP, FDDI SNAP, Token Ring SNAP

- ARPA indicates Ethernet II

- HDLC indicates serial synchronous links

  32 bit network number
 +48 bit node number based on the MAC portion: 24 manufacturer and 24 serial number
 = 80

IPX supports multiple logical networks on a single interface

NOTE:

Novell-ether (raw ether) indicates the Cisco default encapsulation Ethernet 802.3

After version 3.12 Novell uses SAP 802.2)

Cisco Discovery Protocol

- Cisco Discovery Protocol is used to gather and access information about neighboring Cisco devices. However, you cannot configure static routes on a remote router using CDP because you can only gain information about that router.

- CDP uses **advertisements and discovery** methods to learn about their neighbors through Layer 2 multicasting methods and over a SNAP-capable link in order to transmit

- CDP and VTP advertisements are sent out on **VLAN 1**

- CDP uses multicast methods to restrict the discovery process to other Cisco routers

- Cisco routers running CDP discover each other though the use of **SNAP**

Subnetwork Access Protocol at the Data Link layer

- CDP sends out **update** packets **every 60 seconds**, by default

- CDP sends **holdtime** value **every 180 seconds**. The information is discarded if no reply is received.

To view cdp timers and the committed changes
    Router#sh cdp

To increase the cdp timer
    Router(config)#cdp timer [#]

      You can change the cdp timer value from 5-900

To see cdp interface and the encapsulation
    Router#sh cdp int

CDP Problem Area

When you utilize CDP you may encounter a **security risk** for your company. This occurs because the information contained within the router is constantly being broadcast to its neighbors. So, don't hide your mistress; name and telephone number on that router. Also, watch out for the Chinese snoops. They get into everything.

You can disable this security risk to your company and government when you are connected to a non-Cisco router simply by **disabling CDP**.

You can also reduce this terrible, horrendous, consuming risk to soul, limb, and router by turning it off to save on the **router's bandwidth**.

If you are not utilizing the router's bandwidth and not exchanging CDP information, the world is a better and safer place to live.

(Perhaps we should revive letter writing with a trusted courier

NOTE:

CDP is not routable

CDP can, however, because it is by default enabled on all interfaces of the router,
be used to test connectivity issues with other Routers. This permits CDP to troubleshoot.

CDP does not have to be configured through the Network Layer (layer 3)

To enable CDP
    Router(config-if)#cdp run

To disable CDP on an interface
    Router(config-if)#no cdp enable

To see the information received from all routers
    Router#sh cdp entry *   *(requires an asterisk)*

You can also type the specific name of the router you desire to view

    Router#sh cdp entry overthere

To gather information about all the neighbors, as well as device ID, interface platform, holdtime, and port ID

    Router#sh cdp neighbors detail

The Router#sh cdp neighbors presents the following information	
neighbor device ID	name of router to exchange information with
local interface	interface that neighbor is heard on
holdtime	decremental holdtime in seconds
capability	routers capability code

R = router
T = trans Bridge
B = source route bridge
S = switch
H = Host
I = IGMP
r = repeater

Cap R = router   lowercase r = repeater

entry	neighbor entries
interface	status configuration
neighbors	neighbor entries
traffic	statistics

Packet Internet Grouper

$ indicates end of line, continues on next line

.   a period indicates a failed ping

!   Successful   *(UDP uses this)*

U   Unreachable

[ ] Optional

The [   ] can also indicate administrative distance number and the metric number

C   Congested

&   Time to Live exceeded

?   Unknown packet type

- You can PING both the destination and the source IP address

- PING sends multiple IP packets between a sending and a destination device

- Ping checks the IP connection WAN end-to-end in the Network Layer and between two hosts

- Both Ping and Traceroute use ICMP to check the status of other devices and to query the current time

To use IPX to ping

First: you need to know your neighbors address

Router#sh cdp entry

Second, you can type ping followed by the address

Router#ping ipx [ipx network and node address]

Traceroute

- Traceroute provides the IP address and the DNS name of each hop.

- Traceroute is used to troubleshoot the IP connectivity problems between a sending and a destination device

- Traceroute displays each intermediate step as it explores the router path. Trace shows you the last reachable router in the path so you can perform troubleshooting tasks at the approximate location.

P   Protocol Unreachable

N   Network Unreachable

U   Port Unreachable

*   Timeout Occurred

NOTE:

Trace uses UDP packets to discover the next destination hop

Telnet

- Terminal Emulation is an Application Layer Protocol

- You can use Telnet to verify a router's configuration address and to troubleshoot the router's configuration problem

- If you are unable to Telnet the destination, then PING. If you can PING the problem is above the Upper Network layer.

If the PING fails, try Traceroute
    Router#telnet 145.178.123.8
Or
    Router#145.178.123.8

Telnet and PING can be used to verify end-to-end communications

- An ampersand sign (**&**) in a Telnet session indicates that the packet's TTL (Time to live) value was exceeded

- Telnet can be used as a debugging tool because it can impersonate different applications: ie FTP and SMTP

- You use Telnet to test the entire IP stack

To view the multiple simultaneous paths that the router is working with

Router#show sessions

- Because Telnet uses the TCP Protocol it must depend on option negotiation to communicate between the terminal and the mainframe

To deny ALL Telnet traffic from network 8.9.10.0

Router#acces-list 123 deny tcp 8.9.10.0 0.0.0.255. any eq 23

Subnet Mask

Class A	255.0.0.0
Class B	255.255.0.0
Class C	255.255.255.0

- All the bits that are rendered as **1's** in the **network** are the **broadcast** address. They are known as invalid address.

- All the bits that are rendered as **0's** in the **Host** are also broadcast addresses. They also are invalid addresses.

- The IP address borrows bits from the host to create more networks

- The subnet mask is used to determine if an IP address exists on the local network, or outside the local network. Use Boolean algorithm to determine this. 1+1=1, 1+0=0, 0+0=0. This addition process is called ANDING.

To configure
    Router#config t
    Router(config)#int e0
    Router(config-if)#[ip address] [subnet mask]
    Router(config-if)#ctrl + Z
    Router#

You must enter both the IP address and the subnet mask to configure an Ethernet port

To verify
    Router#show int e0

- The IP address is composed of two parts: the network and the host

    The subnet address = network address

    The network portion = the segment

- The network ID requires one allocation for each subnet, and one allocation for each WAN connection.

- The host ID requires an allocation for each router interface. This interface can be composed of computers, network printers, a Unix machine, an Apple machine and, most important, a NIC card.

- The Subnet Mask also considers the number of subnets on your existing network, and the network to come, and the number of current host's ID on each subnet, and the future growth of hosts on the network.

Class	Networks	Hosts / Nodes
A	126	16,777,214
B	16,384	65,382
C	2,097,150	254

- Class A gives you the most hosts, Class C gives you the most networks

- Class C gives you the least hosts, Class A gives you the least networks

Classless Inter-Domain Routing (CIDR)

- CIDR allows router to group routes together so they can reduce the amount of routing information carried by the core routers

- CIDR permits the ISPs to reduce the number of routes carried in their routing tables

- CIDR treats the IP address as classless to permit address aggregation

Bit count formula

0000001 to 1111110 =   1-126   Class A address
1
1000000 to 1011111 = 128-191   Class B address
10
1100000 to 1101111 = 192-223   Class C address
110
1110000 to 1110111 = 224-239   Class D address
1110
1111000 to 1111110 = 240-254   Class E address
1111

127.0.0.1 (0111111) is reserved because it functions as the loopback address

Class C Subnet Chart

Bits	Subnet Mask	Class C Hosts	Subnets	Subnet Range
2	255.192	62	2	64
3	255.224	30	6	32
4	255.240	14	14	16
5	255.248	6	30	8
6	255.252	2	62	4

You need 6 bits to work on a Class C address $2^8 - 2 = 6$

Microsoft uses an additional 2 bits, making theirs a total of 8 bits

7	255.254	*	126
8	255.255	*	254

Microsoft's A and B Classes remain the same

On the subnet range, when you need to calculate it, just add the range number to the preceding number.

When you use the subnet mask of 255.192 the subnet range begins at 64.
Add 64 to 64 = 128. Add 64 to 128 = 192.

When you use the subnet mask of 255.248 the subnet range begins at 8.
Add 8 to 8 = 16. Add 8 to 16 = 24. Add 8 to 24 = 32. etc.

If someone asks you that he has five departments and that he wants you to add another department, this is the same as saying that there are six subnets in the company. Therefore, the maximum growth for each department is 30 computers (nodes / devices) using the subnet of 224.

Subnet Bits

The decimal conversation rate to binary

128	64	32	16	8	4	2	1
1	1	1	1	1	1	1	1

The total of these **8 bits** equals 255, however, when you use the power of 2 the answer becomes 256, necessitating that you subtract one to come to the true answer.

$$128 + 64 + 32 + 16 + 8 + 4 + 2 + 1 = 255$$

You must add an additional one to gain a total of 256 to equal
the statement that the power of two presents to you
$$2^8 x2 = 256$$

If you use the binary BIT number to represent 256 in the power of two, use
$$2^8 = 256$$

$(2^N - 2)$ = # of available subnets
use this formula to calculate the number of hosts

$2^7 - 2 = 128$ subnets
2x2=4=2=8x2=16x2=32=2=64x2=128

Subtract 2
$128 - 2 = 126$

Thus, we can say that $2^7 - 2 = 126$ hosts

2^8	2^7	2^6	2^5	2^4	2^3	2^2	2^1
256	128	64	32	16	8	4	2

[2 X 2 = 4] [4 X 2 = 8] [8 X 2 = 16] [16 X 2 = 32]
2 X 2 X 2 X 2 X 2 X 2 X 2 = 126

Subnetting

- Subnetting reduces the size of the routing table that is stored in the routers by extending and restructuring the existing IP address base.

- To create a subnet, **take a bit from the host** portion of the IP address and give it to the subnet address

- For the Network ID: allocate a bit for each subnet and for each device connection

- For the Device ID: allocate a bit for each TCP/IP host and for each WAN.

- Your entire network organization will get one subnet, and each physical segment of your network will get a subnet number, then make arrangements to allocate a range of host ID, for each subnet that you want to create. After this division, give each device on your segment a 32 bit subnet mask.

Subnetting Example

Example 1

1st Octet								2nd Octet							
255								255							
1	1	1	1	1	1	1	1	1	1	1	1	1	1	1	1
128	64	32	16	8	4	2	1	128	64	32	16	8	4	2	1

3rd Octet								4th Octet / node							
0								0							
0	0	0	0	0	0	0	0	0	0	0	0	0	0	0	**1**
128	64	32	16	8	4	2	1	128	64	32	16	8	4	2	1
								these bits are filled in from the rightmost bit							

Example 2

1st Octet								2nd Octet							
255								255							
1	1	1	1	1	1	1	1	1	1	1	1	1	1	1	1
128	64	32	16	8	4	2	1	128	64	32	16	8	4	2	1

3rd Octet / subnet								4th Octet / node							
128								0							
1	0	0	0	0	0	0	0	0	0	0	0	0	0	0	0
128	64	32	16	8	4	2	1	128	64	32	16	8	4	2	1
these bits are filled in from the leftmost bit															

Example 3

1st Octet								2nd Octet							
255								255							
1	1	1	1	1	1	1	1	1	1	1	1	1	1	1	1
128	64	32	16	8	4	2	1	128	64	32	16	8	4	2	1

3rd and 4th Octet / host device															
0								0							
0	0	0	0	0	0	0	**0**	**0**	0	0	0	0	0	0	0
128	64	32	16	8	4	2	1	128	64	32	16	8	4	2	1
These two center bits are the last to be allocated															

Subnetting Class C

subnet a portion of the IP address in the 4th octet

0							
1	1	0	0	0	0	0	0
128	64	32	16	8	4	2	1

this is filled in from the leftmost bit

$$128 + 64 = 192$$

The two bits in the leftmost side are allocated for the subnet. These leaves 6 bits left over for the host to work with.

Subnet 32 / host portion of the IP address in the 4th octet

0							
0	0	1	0	0	0	0	0
128	64	32	16	8	4	2	1

these bits are filled in after the subnet bits
have been allocated

$16 + 8 + 4 + 2 + 1 = 31$. Add 1 bit to 31 to equal 32.

255.255.255.32

this is the subnet address portion of the IP address

To discover the first valid host ID, add 2 bits to 31 to get **33**. This is the first valid host. **255.255.255.33**

The last valid host is 62. Subtract 2 bits from 64
255.255.255.62

The broadcast address is 63. Subtract 1 bit from 64.
255.255.255.63

NOTE:

To enable a 128 subnet mask, type
Router(config-if)#ip subnet-zero

Five Steps of Subnetting

Discover your number of subnets, discover the broadcast address for each subnet,
discover the number of hosts per subnet, find out what the valid subnet is,
find out what the valid host range is

To discover the number of hosts, we will work with the 4th octet of the Class C address							
$2^X - 2 = x$ we count the 1's of **masked bits** and discover that we have 6 ones and 2 zeros $2^2 - 2$ is the amount of **masked bits** so there are 2 hosts							
1	1	1	1	1	1	0	0
128	64	32	16	8	4	2	1

*(In the above example we used **MASKED** bits)*

To discover the number of hosts per subnet, reverse the order of zeros and ones							
$2^X - 2 = x$ we count the 1's of **unmasked bits** and discover that we have 2 zeros and 6 ones $2^6 - 2$ is the amount of **unmasked** bits so there are 62 subnets per subnet							
1	1	1	1	1	1	0	0
128	64	32	16	8	4	2	1

*In the above example, we used **UNMASKED** bits*

How To Discover the Valid Subnet

To find out what the valid subnet is

There are a total of 256 subnets per octet or to put it in another formula:
there are 8 bits per octet.

A Class A address will have 24 bits
A Class B address will have 16 bits
A Class C address will have 8 bits

(256 total possible amount) [subtract the subnet mask] = {variable}

$$256 - 64 = 192$$

192 is an invalid subnet because it contains all 1's

$$192 - 64 = 128 \quad (255.255.255.128)$$

$$128 - 64 = 64 \quad (255.255.255.64)$$

3 is invalid because it contains all 0's

1	1	1	1	1	1	0	0
128	64	32	16	8	4	2	1

On a 192 subnet mask, the $2^2 - 2$ will always equal 2

How To Discover the Valid Host Range

To find out what the valid host range is							
We eliminate all zeros and all ones and the numbers between the 0's and 1's are the valid hosts all 0's mean "this node"　　all 1's mean "all nodes" The first valid host is 129　and　the last valid host is 190							
1	1	1	1	1	1	0	0
128	64	32	16	8	4	2	1

Discover first the subnet address then the broadcast address.
The hosts will be easier to discover at that point

How To Discover the Broadcast

To discover the broadcast address for each subnet							
First, find out which bits make up all ones Subtract the last number from the total 192 – 1 = 191 191 is the broadcast address							
1	**1**	**1**	**1**	**1**	**1**	**0**	**0**
128	64	32	16	8	4	2	1

*(Always count the bits from the **leftmost** side*
*when you are calculating the number of **subnets**)*

128	64	32	16	8	4	2	1
1	1	1	1	1	1	1	1

*Always count the bits from the **rightmost** side*
*when you are calculating the number of **hosts***

Another Subnetting Method

Question: If you have an IP host of 222.123.4.115 and a subnet of 255.255.255.248, how do you discover the broadcast?

First step

```
 255.255.255.255
-255.255.255.248
=              7
```

Second step:
convert 222.123.4.111 to binary

128	64	32	16	8	4	2	1
1	1	0	1	1	1	1	0

[128 + 64 = 192] [192 – 222 = 30] [16 + 8 = 24] [4 + 2 = 6] = **222**

128	64	32	16	8	4	2	1
0	1	0	1	1	0	1	1

[64 + 32 = 96 + 16 = 112] [112– 123 = 11 – 8 = 2 + 1] = **123**

128	64	32	16	8	4	2	1
0	0	0	0	0	1	0	0

[4 + 0 = 4] = **4**

128	64	32	16	8	4	2	1
0	1	1	0	1	1	1	1

[64 + 32 + 96] [111-96 =15] [8 +4 + 2 + 1 = 15] = **111**

In the third step
you must AND the above binary numbers and establish the result

AND means to add the binary numbers together

1 + 1 = 1, 1 + 0 = 0, 0 + 0 = 0

1st Octet								2nd Octet							
222								123							
128	64	32	16	8	4	2	1	128	64	32	16	8	4	2	1
1	0	0	1	1	0	1	1	0	1	1	1	1	0	1	1
1	1	1	1	1	1	1	1	1	1	1	1	1	1	1	1
AND these together								AND these together							
1	0	0	1	1	0	1	1	0	1	1	1	1	0	1	1
The result is								The result is							
1	0	0	1	1	0	1	1	0	1	1	1	1	0	1	1
which is the same as								which is the same as							
222								123							

3rd Octet								4th Octet							
4								111							
128	64	32	16	8	4	2	1	128	64	32	16	8	4	2	1
0	0	0	0	0	1	0	0	0	1	1	0	1	0	1	1
1	1	1	1	1	1	1	1	1	1	1	1	1	1	1	1
AND these together								AND these together							
0	0	0	0	0	1	0	0	0	1	1	0	1	0	1	1
The result is								The result is							
0	0	0	0	0	1	0	0	0	1	1	0	1	0	1	1
which is the same as								which is the same as							
4								111							

Octet	128	64	32	16	8	4	2	1	total
first	1	1	0	1	1	1	1	0	222
second	0	1	1	1	1	0	1	1	123
third	0	0	0	0	0	1	0	0	4
fourth	0	1	1	0	1	0	1	1	111

111 is the broadcast address
222.123.4.104 through 222.123.4.110 are the valid host
addresses

My Subnetting Preference

Class C Address

Total bit range = 255 + 1 = 256							
128	64	32	16	8	4	2	1
1	1	1	1	1	0	0	0
5 bits = 248 Use these 5 bits for the subnet					use these 3 bits for the host		

subnet range				
64	32	16	8	4
255.192	255.224	255.240	255.248	255.252

234.145.67.0 is the network address / 255.255.255.248 is
the subnet mask
248 = 11111000 in binary

FIRST

how many subnets do we have?

$2^5 - 2 = 30$ subnets
2x2=4x2=8x2=16x2=32 – 2 = 30

SECOND

what is the broadcast address?

to discover this we must add together the subnet range.
add 8 to 8 which equals 16 then subtract 1 which equals 15
then add 8 to 15 = 23
and continue with this method until you reach the last
possible number

THIRD

how many hosts do we have?

$$2^3-2 = 6 \text{ hosts}$$
$$2x2=4x2=8 - 2 = 6$$

add one to the subnet mask
[8 + 1 = 9] [16 + 1 = 17] [24 + 1 = 25] [232 + 1 = 233]
[240 + 1 = 241]

FOURTH

What is the last valid host?

To discover this we must subtract one from the broadcast
address.
[15 – 1 = 14] [23 – 1 = 22] etc

Now we will use subtraction (-) and addition (+) to
discover
the valid hosts and broadcast address

$$256 - 248 = 8$$

[8 + 8 = 16] [8 + 16 = 24] [8 + 24 = 32] [8 + 32 = 48]…[8
+ 232 = 240]

The Shorthand Method of Subnetting

Someone asks you to discover the subnet that host 223.45.67.89/12 is on. To find the answer use this method.

First: We are given the fact that the host is on bit number 12

Remember, we are borrowing these bits from the Submask 255 in the 4th octet

Bit numbers are underneath the decimal numbers							
128	64	32	16	8	4	2	1
0	0	0	0	1	1	0	0
lefthand most 4 bits				working area			
1	1	1	1				
128+64+32+16 = 240 or 4 bits				8 + 4 = 12 or 4 bits			

[The power of $2^8 = 256$] $- 240 = 16$

The valid subnets in multiples of 16 are

16, 32, 48, 64, 80, 96, 112, 128, 144, 160, 176, 192, 208, 224, 240

Subtract 1 from the second subnet, then add 1, then subtract
1
to find the broadcast, the first valid host and the last valid
host

$$32 - 1 = 31$$
this is the broadcast

$$16 + 1 = 17$$
this is the first valid host

$$31 - 1 = 30$$
this is the last valid host

continue until you discover the correct subnet

ANSWER:
it is subnet 80

95 is the broadcast. 81 is the first valid host. 94 is the last
valid host.

Another Shorthand Method of Subnetting

Or, try this other method

Divide the number 89 by 16 to get your answer

89 / 16 = 5

Drop the remainder as we only use whole numbers

5 times 16 = 80

80 is the subnet

NOTE:

The Private address are

10.0.0.0 – 10.255.255.255

172.16.0.0 – 172.31.255.255

192.168.0.0 – 192.168.255.255

How To Discover Hosts

Now this same boss who couldn't figure out how to discover the subnet, wants you to help him find a good method of calculating the expansion for his grand plan of creating room for so many hosts. Thank your lucky stars you don't have a hammer in your hand! (But your honor, he always insists that I do it. He doesn't know a node from a net).

"Molly, I want you to put 25 computers, one color laser printer, and one whatever-you-call-it, in this room, over there by that window. Oh, and Molly, leave room for another ten computers next month."

You get out the pencil and add together what the boss wants.

$$25 + 1 + 1 = 27$$

Then next month 10 more, so that's a total of 37 devices or nodes on a single subnet.

The one thing your boss does know, because you gave him the answer the last week, is that the network address is 223.45.67.0.

First:

How many hosts?

The answer: 37. (We already figured this one out up above)

Second:

What is the working subnet?

We use the power of 2 to discover that $2^6 = 63$

add together $32+16+8+4+2+1 = 63$

Bit numbers are underneath the decimal numbers							
128	64	32	16	8	4	2	1
0	0	1	0	0	1	0	1
lefthand most 2 bits		working area					
128 + 64 = **192** or 2 bits		32 +4 + 1 = 37 or 6 bits					

OR

255.255.255.255
-255.255.255.063
000.000.000.**192**

so, the subnet is 255.255.255.192

Third:

How many bits?

Easy. Just look at the working chart and see that we have 6 bits.

6 bits represent what?

$63 - 1 = 62$ hosts

so we have the ability to expand up to 62 computers along
with extra laser printers,
or several more what's-it-called stuff.

Now, go ask your boss for a raise, and never share this
knowledge with him!

The 240 Subnetting Chart

240 working chart

start with second range number, then after subtracting 1,
place the reduced number underneath the original range number

FIRST add together each range number	subnet	**0**	8	**16**	*24*	32	...	232	240
SECOND subtract 1 from the subnet's second column, then add the amount from the first column	broadcast -1	7	**15**	23	31	<u>**39**</u>	...	239	247
THIRD add 1 from the subnet's first column	first valid host +1	1	9	17	*25*	33	...	233	241
FORTH subtract 1 from the broadcast in the first column	last valid host -1	6	14	22	30	<u>**38**</u>	...	238	247

If you are presented with a scenario that tells you that you will need to calculate a range for an IP address that ends in a zero in the fourth octet, the solution is to present the full range of numbers.

255.255.255.0

The range is 189.123.45.1 – 255.255.255.254

The subnet is 0, the broadcast is 255,
the 1st valid address is 1, the last valid address is 254

Subnetting Chart Problems

When we have only one subnet and it happens to be 128, and we want to add another subnet, we must do this:

First, create a global configuration command:
Router(config-if)#ip subnet-zero

so you can use the 1 bit subnet mask

255.255.255.128

128 working chart		subject	1st column	2nd column
first	You must begin in the second column	subnet	**0**	**128**
second	subtract 1 from the subnet's second column, then add the amount. 127 + 128 = 255	broadcast	**127**	255
third	add 1 from the subnet's first column	first valid host	1	129
forth	subtract 1 from the broadcast in the first column	last valid host	126	254

Add 128 to 127. Add 128 to 1. Add 128 to 126.

FIRST COLUMN	SECOND COLUMN
128 − 1 = 127	128 + 1 = 129
0 + 1 = 1	127 + 128 = 255
127 − 1 = 126	255 − 1 = 254

Class B Subnet Chart

Bits	Subnet Mask	Subnets	Class B Hosts	Subnet Range
2	255.192	2	16,382	64
3	255.224	6	8,190	32
4	255.240	14	4,094	16
5	255.248	30	2,046	8
6	255.252	62	1,022	4
7	255.254	126	510	2
8	255.255	254	254	1
9	255.255.128	510	126	128
10	255.255.192	1,022	62	64
11	255.255.224	2,046	30	32
12	255.255.240	4,094	14	16
13	255.255.248	8,190	6	8
14	255.255.252	16,382	2	4

We will now use the third octet until we reach subnet mask 128. After that, we will use the fourth octet. In rendering the fourth octet, place the number 1 before the number 254. i.e. 255.255.1.32. This rendering may appear as a Class C address, but it is not. It is still a Class B address.

When you calculate a Class **B** address you need to figure on using **14** bits

Don't forget the formula $2^{16} - 2 = 14$ working bits
which equals 16,382 subnets
$2^2 - 2 = 2$ hosts

Class B address

1st and 2nd octet	3rd and 4th octet
network portion of ip address	node portion of ip address
156.123	0.0

(In a subnetting question, the network address is used
to tell you the Class type: A, B, or C)

subnet mask (the fourth octet is turned off until you reach 128)
if it was on we would have to place a 1 – 255 in the 4th octet

1st and 2nd octet	3rd and 4th octet
network portion of subnet mask	node portion of subnet mask
255.255	224.0

First, the number of subnets: 224 = 11100000. We have 11 bits. 2^{11}-2 = 2,046 subnets. We have a remainder of 5 bits (16 – 11 = 5). 2^5 –2 = 30 hosts.

Second, the number of valid subnets: subtract 224 from 256 equals 32.
Add 32 to 32 = 64. 32 + 64 = 96. Etc.

Third, the range of valid hosts: 255.255.224.33-62, [65-94] [224-254]

Fourth, the broadcast:[63] [255]. / Fifth: rearrange the numbers in the bottom chart.

The 224 Subnetting Chart

224 Working Chart

FIRST You must begin in the second column	subnet	32	64	96	128	160	192	224
SECOND subtract 1 from the subnet's second column, then add the amount from the first column	broadcast **-1**	63	95	127	<u>159</u>	191	223	255
THIRD add 1 from the subnet's first column	first valid host **+1**	33	65	*97*	129	161	193	224
FOURTH subtract 1 from the broadcast in the first column	last valid host **-1**	62	94	126	<u>158</u>	190	222	254

Add 32 to 63, and continue incrementing.
Do the same on the third row. Add 32 to 33.
And do the same on the fourth row, add 32 to 62.

(Don't forget the zero)

Subnet 0, broadcast 31, 1st valid address 1, last valid address 30

The 3rd Octet Subnetting of Class B

Yes, a Class B address does have a 255.255.255.0

It has 8 bits, so it has 254 subnets, and 254 hosts, and has a valid range of 1-254

The broadcast ranges from 255.255.1.255 - 255.255.254.255

First host 255.255.1.1 – 255.255.1.254

Last host: 255.255.1.254 – 255.255.254.254

Do you remember the 9th bit in the previous example table under subnets?

It is rendered as 255.255.255.128

It has 9 bits, $2^9 - 2 = 510$ subnets, $2^7 - 2 = 126$ hosts. The 128 subnet mask has a range of 128

Remember, we are working from a total of 16 bits, so 9-16=7

The 192 Subnetting Chart

The case of 255.255.255.192

$2^{10} - 2 = 1022$ subnets and $2^6 - 2 = 62$ hosts
256-192=64. 64+64=128. etc.

192 working chart						
You must begin in the second column	subnet	**0**	64	**128**	*192*	There is, however, a special situation here. The hosts and subnet bits in the third octet must be turned on to make 0 and 192 valid.
subtract 1 from the subnet's second column, then add the amount from the first column	broadcast **-1**	63	**127**	191	255	
add 1 from the subnet's first column	first valid host **+1**	1	65	129	*193*	When they are turned on, the third octet is rendered with as a number one.
subtract 1 from the broadcast in the first column	last valid host **-1**	62	126	190	254	1.64; 1.127; 1.65; 1.126 etc.

Add 64 to 64. Add 64 to 127. Add 64 to 65. Add 64 to 190.

Always increment with the original subnet range.

After the 255.255.255.128 in the Class B address the third octet becomes active. The bits rendered will increase from 9 up to 14. In the Class A the bits will continue on toward 24.

Please refer to the subnet table provided earlier.

Question

What is the broadcast address of a Class C network address ID
using the default subnet mask?
195.123.45.**255**

of a Class B address?
128.123.**255.255**

of a Class A address?
110.**255.255.255**

255.255.255.255 = broadcast. Same as all 1's

The 24 bits of Class A

When you calculate a Class **A** address you need to figure on **24** bits

Bits	Subnet Mask	Subnets	Class A Hosts	Subnet Range
2	255.192	2	16,777,208	64
3	255.224	6	8,388,208	32
4	255.240	14	4,194,302	16
5	255.248	30	2,097,150	8
6	255.252	62	1,048,574	4
7	255.254	126	524,286	2
8	255.255	254	262,142	1
9	255.255.128	510	131,070	128
10	255.255.192	1,022	65,534	64
11	255.255.224	2,046	32,767	32
12	255.255.240	4,094	16,382	16
13	255.255.248	8,190	8,190	8
14	255.255.252	16,382	4,094	4

15	255.255.254	32,767	2,046	2
16	255.255.255	65,534	1,022	1
17	255.255.255.128	131,070	510	128
18	255.255.255.192	262,142	254	64
19	255.255.255.224	524,286	126	32
20	255.255.255.240	1,048,574	62	16
21	255.255.255.248	2,097,150	30	8
22	255.255.255.252	4,194,302	14	4
23	255.255.255.254	8,388,604	6	2
24	255.255.255.255	16,777,208	2	1

The usual configuration for the Class A address is to allocate as having

16,777,208 subnets and 126 hosts / networks.

The 32 Bits of Class A

You can also realize the bit values up to 32

Bits	Subnet Mask	Subnets	Range
25	255.255.128	33,554,416	128
26	255.255.192	67,108,832	64
27	255.255.224	134,216,400	32
28	255.255.240	268,435,200	16
29	255.255.248	536,870,040	8
30	255.255.252	1,073,740,800	4
31	255.255.254	2,147,481,600	2
32	255.255.255	4,294,963,200	1

NOTE
The 1st octet of a class A address only uses 7 bits, not 8

1st Octet								2nd Octet							
126								255							
128	64	32	16	8	4	2	1	128	64	32	16	8	4	2	1
0	1	1	1	1	1	1	1	1	1	1	1	1	1	1	1

the leftmost bit + the continuous rightmost bits = 126
which is a Class A address

8 bits = 256, which is an invalid designated address

The 128 Subnetting Chart

You have 22 bits to create a subnet with: 255.0.0.0

$$(2^{24} - 2 = 22)$$

When you use the 255.255.0.0 you have 8 bits to subnet with

When you use 255.255.248.0 you have 13 bits to subnet with

When you use 255.255.255.128 you have 17 bits to subnet with

Use the same formulas as you did on the Class C and B addressing schemes

128 working chart					
You must begin in the second column	subnet	0	255.255 .64	**255.255 .128**	**192**
subtract 1 from the subnet's second column, then place under the first column	broadcast **-1**	**63**	**255.255 .127**	255.255 .191	255
add 1 from the subnet's first column	first valid host **+1**	**1**	255.255 .65	255.255 .129	193
subtract 1 from the broadcast in the first column	last valid host **-1**	**62**	**255.255 .126**	255.255 .190	254

Large Area Network

Protocols

- FDDI
- Token Ring 802.5
- ATM
- HSSI: High-Speed Serial Interface
- SIP: SMDS Interface Protocol
- PPP

- X.25
- HDLC
- SDLC
- LAPB
- SLIP

To see the physical and logical aspects which works at the data-link layer

Router#show interface

- Carrier Detect Signals triggers a line status that can be verified

  Used by show interface command

- Keepalive frames triggers the line protocol

- LAN falls under Data Link layer

WAN Protocol Technologies

ATM	Asynchronous Transfer Mode	packet-switched
Frame Relay	uses PVCs	packet switched
ISDN	Integrated Serial Digital Network	Circuit switched
HDLC	point to point / multipoint	packet switched
SDLC	Synchronous Data Link Control	packet switched
SMDS	Switched Multimegabit Data Service	packet switched
PPP	Point-to-Point	
HSSI	High Speed Serial Interface	
X.25	used on unreliable WAN connections: Africa, Central America. Uses error correction.	packet switched

SDLC

Several hosts can communicate to a dedicated facility

SMDS

One host must be labeled as the primary host while another is labeled as the secondary host

All transmission goes through the primary host

The X.25 protocol uses a Switch between two PDN's

Point-to-Point Protocol

- PPP is a WAN Protocol

- HDLC, LCP *(MAC Sublayer)* and NCP *(LLC Sublayer)* support PPP

- PPP can negotiate, establish and configure different network parameters through NCP: Network Control Protocol

- PPP supports authentication, has link monitoring capability, and allows transfer from several protocols to be **multiplexed** across the link.

- The compression Protocols for PPP are **Stacker, Predictor, and MPPC**

- *Router(config-if)#compress [predictor | stac | mppc {ignore pfc}]*

- PPP uses IPCP (IP Control Protocol) to establish and configure IP's and to assign the IP addresses

- The Multilink Protocol provides **load balancing** across PPP's multiple paths

- The Link Quality Management Protocol (LQM) is used for **error detection** and to monitor **dropped data packets.** LQM also analyzes the percentage of lost packets.

- The Magic Number avoids frame dropping

- PPP supports IPX and DECnet

- PPP can operate across any DTE/DCE interface

  To do this, PPP requires a duplex switch

- PPP is a dial-up protocol

- PPP can be configured as a connectionless protocol

- PPP can encapsulate multiple protocols over a dialup connection as well as from a LAN to LAN leased line

- PPP is NOT a networking standard for transmitting info over a physical medium

  Compression Protocols for PPP: Stacker, Predictor, and MPPC

To configure PPP on a router

    Router#config t
    Router(config)#username Molly password WhyEnter
    Router(config)#interface e0
    Router(config-if)#encapsulation ppp
    Router(config-if)#^+Z
Or
    Router(config if)#encap ppp
same as
    Router(config-if)#encapsulation [hdlc | ppp | lapb]

Do not confuse encapsulation ppp
with
ppp authentication that is used to enable CHAP and PAP

To monitor PPP activity
    Router#show interface
Or
    Router#debug ppp chap   *(or pap)*

Link Control Protocol

- LCP (Link Control Protocol) is the protocol responsible for a PPP connection. It establishes, configures, negotiates, tests, maintains, and terminates PPP connections through the WAN link

LCP establishes, configures, tests, maintains, and terminates
PPP connections through

1	Link establishment
2	Link Maintenance
3	Link Termination Parameters

Challenge Handshake Authentication Protocol (CHAP)

- CHAP performs a three-way handshake when PPP tries to establish communication with another node

- CHAP uses MD5 hushing to protect the password parameters

CHAP can adversely affect the capability of a Web server by overloading it

CHAP uses a variable challenge value that is unique and unpredictable to authenticate the packet's origination

To enable CHAP
Router(config-if)#ppp authentication chap

You must be in interface configuration command to enable CHAP and PAP

To view CHAP communication exchanges
Router#debug ppp authentication

To **stop** viewing the exchanges, use the undebug command
Router#undebug ppp authentication
Same as
Router#debug ppp [authentication | pap | chap | compression | error | multilink | negotiation | packet | tasks]

Password Authentication Protocol
(PAP)

- PAP's username and passwords are transmitted in clear text.

- A remote laptop computer (or node / device) can initiate the PAP authentication process

- PAP can be used to connect AppleTalk servers to its clients

To enable PAP
    Router(config-if)#ppp authentication pap

Integrated Services Digital Network (ISDN)

- ISDN uses **circuit switching** to establish a dedicated circuit path between the sender and the receiver

- This digital telephony service will one day provide the world with high-speed imaging capabilities over a digital modem, along with file transfers and stream video downloading. Can't wait to get it at home!

- ISDN uses LAPB as its signaling protocol

ISDN uses the below standards, as defined by ITU

- I = concepts, interfaces, and terminology

- E = existing telephone lines

- Q = switching and signaling.

  Q is also referred to as "Setup and Tear-Down"

NOTE:

Q.921 = Data-Link Layer

Q.931 = Network Layer

Q.921 and Q.931 functions under the Q reference standard.

To verify connectivity to the telco's ISDN switch
    Router#debug isdn q921

To configure ISDN on your router
    Router#config t
    Router(config)#isdn switch-type [switch type]
    Router(config)#dialer-list [dialer-group] protocol
[protocol-name] permit
    Router(config)#interface bri 0
    Router(config-if)#**encapsulation ppp**
    Router(config-if)#dialer-group [number]
    Router(config-if)#dialer map [protocol] [next-hop
address] name [host name] speed [number] [dialer-string]
    Router(config-if)#dialer idle-timeout [seconds]

The dialer-list is used to determine interesting traffic

The dialer-group binds the access list to an ISDN number

LAPD works on the D channel of ISDN Bri

whereas

**ISDN B Bri channels
support the encapsulation types of HDLC, LAPB, and
PPP**

*HDLC is the default encapsulation on an ISDN BRI
interface*

B = bearer channels. D = signaling channels

ISDN Bearer Channels

Primary Rate ISDN (PRI) for the US and Japan
23B + 1D channels of 64Kbps each
for a total of
1.54 **Mbps** otherwise known as a T1 line
Capital M = megabits   a period is used after the one

The T1 line is the default bandwidth of a serial connection

Basic Rate ISDN (BRI) for the US and Japan
2B+1D channels consists of
2 64Kbps signaling lines
and
1 16Kbps administrative line
for a total of 144 **kbps**
(lowercase k = kilobits,   no period after the one)

ISDN connection begins at 64kbps

*128 kbps is the maximum data transfer and connection
speed for an ISDN BRI service*

Of course, we can't forget the Europeans and the Australians. Their **E1** ISDN transmission rate is 2.048 Mbps. Europe's PRI is 30 B channels with 1 64 kbps D channel. Do the Europeans and Aussies demand faster service to have more time for fun?

To view the status of channel 1 on Bri 0
　　Router#show interface bri0:1　　　　*(this argument works with* a　:　*colon)*

- ISDN also implements multiprotocol support, SNMP MIB support, call screening, (Yes dear, don't pretend you aren't calling me nasty things when you're in Rome because I know it's you.)

- ISDN can also utilize compression techniques through the usage of Stacker and Predictor.

- Compression will increase the throughput (overhead) of the router

- ISDN uses digital lines and is implemented as a **dial-up** service on the telephone network

- A CSU/DSU device is also used when communicating over digital lines

The ISDN uses the CSD/DSU to interface with the digital lines

- It is best to use static lines with ISDN

ISDN will one day replace POTS (analog phone lines

Frame-Relay will one day replace X.25

To see information about ISDN statistics
Router#show ISDN statistics

- ISDN Function represents devices or hardware in ISDN

- You can connect up to 8 devices on a single ISDN line to share the ISDN bandwidth.

(Fax machines, routers, terminal adapters, etc)

To monitor ISDN or DDR
Router#show interface
Or
Router#show controllers
Or
Router#show dialer

To set up call screening
Router(config-if)#isdn caller [telephone number]

ISDN SERVICE PROFILE ID
(ISDN SPID)

- Service Profile ID is used between your ISDN equipment and the telephone company's switch.

- The SPID number is provided by the telephone company or by the Service Provider

- The SPID is a unique identifier number

When configuring BRI ISDN on a router, each B channel should be assigned a SPID (Service Profile Identifier). The SPID is provided by the ISP or the telephone company, and can be specified on the router by using the ISDN SPID [spidnumber] command.

To configure BRI ISDN on 2 B channels
    Router#config t
    Router(config)# int bri0
    Router(config-if)#isdn spid 1 1234567
    Router(config-if)#isdn spid 2 1234678
    Router(config-if)#[ip address] [subnet mask]
    Router(config-if)#no shutdown
    Router(config-if)#^Z
    Router#

Three methods to verify an ISDN connection
    Router#show isdn status
Or
    Router#ping
Or
    Router#show dialer

ISDN Reference Points

A reference point is an interface between a variety of groups. The reference points indicates the cabling between the devices.

R	TE2 and TA	non-ISDN and TA
S	TE1 and NT2	user terminal and NT2
T	NT1 and NT2	NT1 and NT2 devices
U	NT1 and LT	NT1 and Line Termination

The LT terminates the local loop.

The NT1 is built into the U interface

S and T are usually combines

S/T = 4 wires

U = 2 wires

NOTE:

A TE1 device = interface [bri interface] number

A DDR = dialer-list [dialer-group] protocol [permit]

TE1 & TE2

- TE1 is used for ISDN. A TE1 understands what a native digital ISDN telephone is. A TE1 has a built-in analog to digital converter.

- A TE1 has a built in BRI connector on the router

PC or Digital Telephone	NT2	T	NT1	U	ISDN Switch or LT

TE2

- A TE2 requires a TA for its BRI signals

- The DTE (Data Terminating Equipment) is a TE2 device

- A TE2 is an analog device that will NOT SUPPORT digital ISDN

A TE1 is a device that has a built-in BRI so it already transmits BRI signals
versus
A TE2 which does NOT have a built-in BRI

Analog Telephone	R	TA	S	NT2	T	NT1	U	ISDN Switch or LT

NOTE:

ISDN modem = TA

ISDN telephone = TE1

278

NT1

- The NT1 converts a BRI signal for use by the ISDN line

- If the router has a BRI interface, attach it to the NT1

- If you want a BRI to stay up during a power outage, you must supply a UPS *(Uninterrupted Power Supply)* to the NT1

Non-ISDN Device	R	**TA**	T	**NT1**	U	ISDN Switch or LT

- ISDN Terminal Adapters Can be used to make analog phone calls over digital lines

- Has one port for the ISDN phone line and one port for the computer or router

- Has ports for fax machines

- Uses a EIA/TIA 232 cable

- Outside the United States, the NT1 is provided to the customer by the telephone company *(Telco)*

- If your router does not have a built in BRI, you need a **NT1** and a **TA** device to connect to the ISDN service

An ISDN BRI interfaces with a NT1 device
whereas
An ISDN PRI interfaces with a CSU/DSC device

- A CSU/DSU (channel service unit/data service unit) is a device required by a router to transmit and receive data from a Frame Relay network link.

CSU: Channel Service Unit is a device that is used to connect
end-user equipment to the local digital telephone loop

DSU: Data Service Unit is used to adapt the physical interface
on a DTE device to a T1 circuit. DSU also performs the signaling timing

NT2 & TA

- The NT2 uses PBX devices to support on-premises ISDN concentration

TA

- You need a TA to convert the serial signal from your router into a BRI signal

- You need a NT1 to connect the BRI signal for use by the ISDN digital line

- A TA converts the **serial signals** to BRI signals

- With a TA, a router or device, can connect to an NT1 device

- A TA converts RS-232 and a V.35 into BRI signals

- The TA is referred to as the **native** ISDN modem

HDLC

- HDLC is a synchronous serial link protocol that uses frame characters and checksums

- HDLC functions under the Layer 2 Protocol (Data-Link Layer)

- HDLC is a **point-to-point protocol used on leased lines**

synchronous serial links

HDLC does not need to be authenticated

To encapsulate hdlc on a serial link   *(hdlc is the default)*
        Router#config t
        Router(config)#int s0
        Router(config-if)#encapsulation hdlc
same as
        Router(config-if)#encapsulation [hdlc | ppp | lapb]

If it is necessary for you to connect to a non-Cisco router, you must use the PPP protocol or Frame-Relay

HDLC supports three transfer modes		
NRM	Normal Response Mode	permission is required from the secondaries to communicate with the primaries
ARM	Asynchronous Transfer Mode	secondary can communicate with the primary
ABM	Asynchronous Balance Mode	can communicate with either

NOTE:

The LAPB (Link Access Protocol, Balanced) is restricted to the ABM.

An LAPB can be activated with the DTE or DCE device.

Frame Relay

A WAN protocol

- Frame Relay is a dynamic connection-oriented protocol that preestablishes its link before sending its data. It is also a **packet-switching** technology that is replacing X.25

X.25 uses PVC's and resides in the Data-Link Layer

- Frame Relay sends data over WAN links through the use of **logical circuits**

Virtual Circuits create a bi-directional communication path from
one DTE device to another DTE device

- The Frame Relay can create a Virtual Circuit between 2 DTE devices

- The Frame Relay Virtual Circuit uses SVCs and PVCs

- Frame Relay data is encapsulated into packets

An ISP is used to route the packets through a variety of switching points

- Frame Relay supports IETF and CISCO (default) frame types for encapsulation.

ISDN will one day replace POTS (analog phone lines)

Frame-Relay will one day replace X.25

- Frame Relay is a Data-Link Layer protocol **that handles multiple virtual circuits** using HDLC (High-Level Data Link Control) encapsulation between the connected devices

Frame Relay Packet				
Flags	10 bit DLCI address	data	FCS	Flag

To tell your router to perform Frame Relay switching
    Router#config t
    Router(config)#frame-relay switching

To configure the Frame Relay
    Router#config t
    Router(config)#int s0
    Router(config-if)#encap frame-relay
    Router(config-if)#frame relay intf-type dce

intf-type dce tells the router to perform DCE
communications
(use one hyphen)

To identify the PVC (Private Virtual Circuit) on a DLCI virtual circuit
    Router#config t
    Router(config)#int s0
    Router(config-if)#frame-relay interface-dlci [#]

*Two hyphens   /   the **dlci** # makes this a **Data-Link layer***

***

To set the frame relay interface s0 bandwidth to 56kbps
    Router(config)#interface s0
    Router(config-if)#bandwidth 56

To enable Inverse ARP
    Router(config-if)#frame-relay inverse-arp [protocol] [dlci]

IARP exchanges ARP messages every 60 seconds

- Frame Relay provides digital communication for packet-switched networks, multiple WANs via single connection

- A packet switching device shares a single point-to-point link to transport packets from a source to a destination across an ISP's network

To configure Frame Relay on serial0 interface using the default encapsulation type
    Router(config)#int s0
    Router(config-if)#encapsulation frame-relay cisco
This is the same as
    Router(config-if)#encapsulation frame-relay

To configure Frame Relay and connect it to an ISP that does not use a CISCO router

    Router(config)#int e1
    Router(config-if)#encapsulation frame-relay ietf

***

Two methods to see PVC statistics and configured DLCI's
And
To see the active connections on each interface and subinterface

    Router#show frame pvc
Or
    Router#show running-config

To monitor the static and dynamic mappings
And
To view the mapping

    Router#sh int s0
Or
    Router#sh frame-relay map

Don't forget: in order to use the Frame Relay map command
you must specify both an IP address and a DLCI

To create a Frame Relay map

    Router(config-if)#frame-relay map [protocol] [protocol address] [dlci]
[broadband] [ietf | cisco | payload compress packet-by-packet]

To change the keepalive message interval

    Router(config-if)#keepalive [# of seconds]

The keepalive default time is every 10 seconds

Congestion Detection Methods

FECN

Forward Explicit Congestion Notification

- FECN is the bit in the data inside a Frame Relay's header packet that detects congestion on a route, and transmit that info forward to the receiving Switch or DTE

A Frame Relay packet uses a FECN bit to notify the destination device that there is too much activity on it. The FECN notification temporarily delays the forwarding process until the destination device is able to receive more packets

BECN

Backward Explicit Congestion Notification

The BECN bit inside the Frame Relay header packet tells the source router to slow down the transmission of the Frame Relay packets

Committed Information Rate & DE

- CIR guarantees a minimum bandwidth.

- A Committed Burst (Bc) allows you to exceed the CIR for a brief moment

- The Committed Information Rate (Tc) is the agreed transfer data rate

The Local Access Rate is the clock speed of the local loop to the Frame Relay cloud.

This is the rate at which data travels into or out of the network

NOTE:

The DTE is faster than the CIR

DE

Discard Eligibility

This is also a bit that is in the Frame Relay header that signals a Switch that if it must begin a discarding process, to discard the frames that are encoded with the DE bit.

Data-Link Connection Identifier (DLCI)

frame-relay map protocol protocol-address DLCI
[broadcast] [ietf | cisco]

Cisco is the default

- DLCI identifies the logical connection made with Frame Relay, so a DLCI number is required on each Frame Relay circuit

- DLCI is a unique number used to identify a Frame Relay connection

- DLCI is a unique number assigned to map an IP address to a PVC

The PVC creates the logical link between two DTE devices

- In Basic Frame Relay DLCI's are locally significant

- DLCI resides in the Data-Link layer

For example DLCI 1050 is a Data Link layer number

To see what the configured DLCI numbers are on a Frame Relay router
    Router#show running-config
Or
    Router#show run
Or
    Router#sh frame-relay pvc

To see the associated local DLCI for each remote destinations
Or
To see the list of all layer 3 to layer 2 mappings for Frame Relay

    Router#show frame-relay map

To see the serial interfaces that a multicast DLCI is using and the LMI
used for local management

    Router#show interface serial

configured = show
associated = mapping

Two methods to map an IP address to a DLCI use
and
To assign the Layer 3 address to a Layer 2 Frame Relay DLCI

    Router(config-if)#**inverse arp**
Or

    Router(config-if)#**frame-relay map ip** 123.156.7.1
234

The command to map an IP address to a DLCI is based on this argument
Router(config-if)frame-relay interface dlci [statement]

234 is a DLCI value

You must map an IP address to the DLCI
in order to communicate over a virtual circuit

To do so, type
    Router(config-if)#frame-relay interface-dlci [#]

The map configuration is
    Router#config t
    Router(config)#int s0
    Router(config-if)#encap frame
    Router(config-if)#int s0.7 [multipoint | point-to-point]
    Router(config-if)#**inverse-arp**
    Router(config-if)#[ip address] [subnet mask]
    Router(config-if)#**frame-relay map** [ip address] [dlci
#] cisco

To see the DLCI line speed
    Router#show interface

To configure DLCI 123 on interface e0
    Router#conf t
    Router(config)#int e0
    Router(config-if)#frame-relay local-dlci 123

Inverse ARP

- Inverse ARP is used to dynamically map an IP address to the DLCI number

- Inverse ARP works with LMI to resolve the IP address from a DLCI number

- IARP is used by the local router on the network to discover another router and quickly introduce itself to that remote router at the end of the other connection.

  IARP identifies two end points to each other

To turn off dynamic IARP
    Router(config-if)#no inverse-arp

Sometimes you must configure the address-to-DLCI table manually. You do this when you want to control the broadcast traffic, or when you are using OSPF over Frame Relay, and when the remote router can not support Inverse ARP.

To see the Inverse ARP information
    Router#debug frame-relay events

NOTE:

Dynamic = IARP

Manual = map command

293

Local Management Interface (LMI)

- LMI uses three signaling formats *(types)* to manage a Frame Relay connection

    1. CISCO = default
    2. ANSI
    3. Q933A

To configure a router to use any of these three signaling methods *(types)*
    Router#config t
    Router(config)#int e0
    Router(config-if)#frame-relay lmi-type [cisco | ansi | q933a]

After version 11.2 LMI can **autodetect** / **autosense** the LMI signaling format

To obtain information about LMI statistics
    Router#show frame lmi

- LMI is a set of enhancements to the basic Frame Relay specification.

- LMI includes support for a keepalive mechanism, which verifies that data is flowing

    Router(config-if)#keepalive [number of seconds]

- Also, LMI uses a multicast mechanism which provides the network server with its local DLCI and the multicast DLCI

    (LMI uses DLCI 1023)

294

- LMI is used for global addressing schemes, for multicasting, and for maintaining virtual circuit status message for exchanging communication between the DTE and the DCE

- LMI gives the DLCI a unique global address rather than just local significance

- LMI uses Inverse ARP to resolve an IP address from a DLCI number

- LMI provides global addressing which gives DLCI global rather than local significance in a Frame Relay network

- LMI uses Subinterfaces to allow you to route an IP on a single virtual circuit and also to route IPX at the same time on another **virtual circuit**

- LMI provides a status mechanism which gives an on-going (current) status report on the DLCI's known to the switch. the status of virtual circuits, and the global or local significance of the DLCI values

To resolve an IP address for a DLCI number use Inverse ARP

To set the LMI type on a serial interface
Router#sh frame-relay lmi

To view LMI messages that describe LMI flow
Router#debug frame-relay lmi

Dial-on Demand Routing (DDR)

Dial-on demand routing is used to provide access to wide area networks (WAN) links. DDR must use static routes.

- DDR can be used to find interesting traffic **as defined by the access lists**

In order to specify the types of interesting traffic, you must use a subinterface for each type of traffic

- **Static routes** must be used because DDR is not active at all times

Static routes inform the router where to forward packets

Static routes do not activate a DDR connection

To create a static route
    Router(config)#ip route [network] [subnet mask] [IP address] [distance]
    Router(config)#ip route 198.123.45.0 255.255.255.0 123.45.67.80 9

This sends all packets destined for network 198.123.45.0 to router 123.45.67.8

Connect the DDR to the auxiliary port on the back of the router

You must specify the **interesting traffic** for DDR

- ISDN can be used with DDR as well as X.25 and Frame Relay

- DDR can function as a **backup** to a primary WAN connection

- DDR can provide access to locations where WAN usage is infrequent

- **DDR should not be used in high-volume sites**

- DDR triggers a router to initiate the WAN connection

To monitor DDR
And
To see the total link time connections
    Router#show dialer

To configure DDR you must

1) define the static route,

2) specify the internetwork traffic,

3) and configure the dialer parameter

To see the current status of a legacy DDR connection
    Router#show isdn status

Subinterfaces

To configure a subinterface to Ethernet_802.2
    int e1.222
    ipx networkB222 encap sap 222

You must use the period . before the number in the
***interface** command line*

To configure e0 on the router to use an IPX subinterface
and to encapsulate Ethernet_802.2 on the same network

    Router#config t
    Router(config)#int e0.99
    Router(config-if)#ipx network 99 encapsulation sap
    Router(config-if)#ctrl + Z   *(^+Z)*
    Router#

To support both Novell Ethernet_802.3 and 802.2 frame
types on a network, you must add the Cisco SAP
encapsulation to the router interface that supports Ethernet

To create a single ethernet interface so it will permit both
SAP and novel-ether encapsulation
    Router(config t
    Router(config)#int e1.90
    Router(config-if)#ipx encapsulation novell-ether
    Router(config-if)#ipx network 1a
    Router(config-if)#int e1.99
    Router(config-if)#ipx encapsulation sap
    Router(config-if)#ipx network 2b

NOTE:

You can also configure the subinterface on an IP address

To do this: first, disable the layer 3 address. Second, enable Frame Relay encapsulation.

```
Router#config t
Router(config)#int e0
Router(config-if)#encapsulation frame-relay
Router(config-if)#no ip address
Router(config-if)#^Z
Router#
```

To add more frame types to interface e0
```
Router(config)#int e0
Router(config-if)#ipx network 22a encap sap sec
Router(config-if)#int e0.5
Router(config-subif)#ipx network 22b encap arpa
Router(config-subif)#int e0.51
Router(config-subif)#ipx network 22c encap snap
```

and so forth

Commit the secondary command before you begin the other interfaces. Please note that the command interface has changed to **subif** from if.

Virtual Local Area Network (VLAN)

- A VLAN is a logical grouping of devices that function independently of the physical layout of a network

- Administrative duties are lessened because if you want to move Molly's computer to your office because you got a thing for her, you can do it without having to reconfigure her computer through the head-honcho of the IT department. It'll just be our secret she's now in your office performing those personal tidbits. Yeah, dream-on!

Members of each VLAN function as totally separate networks

- By default all nodes on a network are members of the same VLAN

Any broadcast frame sent by a particular VLAN member will be propagated only to the members of that VLAN

- Each VLAN is assigned a unique number

- VLANs can be used to improve network performance

- VLANs increase security in a network

- VLANs decrease network traffic

- VLANs assign users to a specific LAN on a port-by-port basis versus on a device basis

   You can easily add or remove a user to a VLAN by going through the port-by-port parameters

   You add or delete a user by making a software configuration change in the switch and by assigning the user's port to a new VLAN

- Users on the same VLAN do not have to be connected to the same device

- The maximum amount of VLANS that you can create is switch dependent

VLANs break up broadcast domains in a switched internetwork

versus

Layer 2 switches, which can only break up collision domains

By default, all switches make up one long broadcast domain

Microsegmentation is the process of creating multiple VLANs on a single physical network into multiple physical networks

To divide a single physical network into multiple VLANs use microsegmentation

Static VLANs are more most secure than Dynamic VLANs

To create a VLAN with the ID number 0099 and assign the name Molly to this VLAN
    Router(config)#vlan 0099 name Molly
Or
    Router(config)#vlan [vlan ID] [name {vlan_name}]

To see the VLAN names, status, assigned ports, type, and VLAN configuration information
    Router#show vlan

To see the VLAN assignment and membership types for all switch ports
    Router#show vlan-membership static [vlan]

VLAN0001, 1002, 1003, 1004, 1005 are created by default.

There is no VLAN1001

If no name is specified for a VLAN, than the default name is VLAN [ID]

Users in a VLAN share the same broadcast domain. The cable, segment, or subnet may be separated geographically.

VLAN Frame Tagging

- Frame tagging is the process used by switches to identify a computer's VLAN membership. Many Army generals frame-tag their subordinate's careers.

- Frame tagging = The VLAN tag is renamed before exiting the Trunk Links

- Once the frame reaches an exit to an Access link, the switch **removes** the VLAN identifier (VLAN ID)

- Tagging allows VLANs to be multiplexed over a Trunk Line through an external encapsulation method

VLAN ISL

- The ISL (Inter-Switch Link) encapsulates a frame with a new header and CRC information

A virtual circuit must connect two DTE devices within a Frame Relay network

- Frame tagging can maintain a VLAN across multiple switches and through an **Inter-Switch Link (ISL)**

Trunks are used to carry VLAN information between switches

- When a frame travels over a Trunk Link, it is encapsulated in ISL information. The ISL information is removed before the frame is sent down an Access link

- The Trunk and ISL are used to configure trunking on a switch

- When you establish a new VLAN you are also creating a new Broadcast domain. This means this: when you have formed this new entity, you will also increase the number of broadcast domains. But **no**, you are NOT increasing the number, nor decreasing the number, of **collision domains.**

- ISL provides low latency, at full **wire-speed** performance over Fast Ethernet when using half-duplex or full-duplex mode

- ISL VLAN information is added to a frame only if the frame is forwarded out a port configured over a Trunk Link

- The ISL encapsulation is removed from the frame if the frame is forwarded out an Access link

- To **identify** the VLAN that a frame belongs to with ethernet technology, use **ISL** and **802.1q**

Inter-Switch Link in General Terms

- ISL and frame tagging are used to **connect to multiple switches** and maintain VLAN identification for traffic passing between the switches.

- When a frame leaves one switch for another, it uses frame tagging and ISL

- The first switch encapsulates the frame with an ISL header that *tags* the frame with a user-defined VLAN ID

- ISL is used only by Fast Ethernet and by Gigabit Ethernet links

- An ISL header is 26 bytes long. It also uses a 4 byte long FCS

The ISL can be used to extend the size of an Ethernet frame

- The ISL frame is 1522 frames long

Keyword
Functional Area

VLAN VMPS

VLAN Management Policy Server

- Dynamic VLANs are created through the VMPS

- A VLAN Management Policy Server (VMPS) must be configured with the hardware address of all hosts on the internetwork

- The VMPS sets up a database of MAC addresses that can be used for dynamic addressing of VLANs

- VMPS is a MAC address-to-VLAN mapping database

VLAN VTP

Virtual Trunk Protocol

- VLAN VTP is a layer 2 messaging protocol (Data-Link)

- The Virtual Trunk Protocol (VTP) is used to propagate VLAN information across a Trunk Link

- VTP Pruning enables the switching fabric to prevent flowing traffic problems on the trunk port

- VTP can help you have a stable, consistent VLAN database in all your servers by managing the Administrative router of its domain

- All Cisco switches are VTP by default

- VTP is used if you have multiple switches and your network has multiple VLANs configured

VTP benefits to a switched network

- Management of all switches and routers in an internetwork

- Consistency of VLAN configuration across all switches in the network

- Allows VLANs to be Trunked over mixed networks, like ethernet to FDDI

- Accurate trunking and monitoring of VLANs

- Dynamic reporting of added VLANs to all switches

- Plug-and-Play configuration in the VLAN environment

- To use VTP: first, create the VTP server. Second, create a domain name

A switch can only be in one domain at a time.
A switch can only share VTP domain information with switches
configured in the same VTP domain

- VTP information is sent between switches via a Trunked port

- Every switch must have the same password

- The higher the revision number, the more current the information. You can overwrite the current database with new information

- To preserve VTP broadband: use VTP Pruning. VTP Pruning must be enabled on the switch

- VTP allows VLANs to be Trunked over mixed networks. Ethernet to ATM Lane or FDDI

- VTP (VLAN Trunking Protocol) operates in the **server, client, and transparent mode**

- VTP advertisements are sent every 5 minutes

- VTP is a Layer 2 messaging protocol that maintains VLAN configuration consistency throughout a common administrative domain

- VTP minimizes misconfiguration and duplication of VLAN names

To reset the VTP configuration revision number on a switch
   Router#delete vtp

To create a VTP domain named Molly on a switch
   Router(config)#vtp domain Molly

The VTP command is used to enable or disable traps and prunning

This is the entire command
   Router(config)#vtp [server | transparent | client {domain-name}] [trap {enable | disable}] [password {password}] [pruning {enable | disable}]

To have the VTP create, modify, and delete VLANS in the Server and Transparent modes
   Router(config)#vtp transparent domain Molly

Use Transport Mode

To see the maximum number of VLANs supported, the VTP version of the VLAN, the number of existing VLANs, and the VTP configuration information, type:

   Router#show vtp

VLAN VTP Pruning

- VTP Pruning is disabled by default on all switches

- When VTP Pruning is enabled it is enabled for the entire domain. Only VLANs 1002-1005 are pruning-eligible.

- VLAN 1 can never be pruned as it is an Administrative VLAN

- VTP Pruning blocks VLAN traffic to switches that don't have ports assigned to the VLAN.

- VTP Pruning prevents traffic flooding by discarding useless traffic on the trunk ports by eliminating the data destined for VLANs that are not configured on the destination switch

VLAN Trunking

Trunking Concepts

- **Trunking** is the process of making a computer a member of multiple VLANs

- For VLANs to span multiple switches, a trunk connection must be established

- Any Fast Ethernet or ATM (Asynchronous Transfer Mode) port on a catalyst switch can become the designated trunk port.

You must use a 100BaseT cable connected to an ISL ethernet card

- By default, if you create a Trunk Link, all VLANs are allowed on that Trunk Link. You must delete any unwanted VLANs manually

- By utilizing the Trunking services, a server can be in two broadcast domains at the same time. Moreover, users do not have to use a router to login to use the server

- A Trunk Link can carry, on a point-to-point basis, multiple VLANs.

- Trunk Links are used to connect switches to other switches, to routers and to servers.

- The Trunk Link can only use Fast Ethernet or Gigabit Ethernet

- If a Trunk Link fails, it will report to a native *(default)* VLAN

- Trunking allows you to send information about VLANs across one link

To see the DISL and Fast Ethernet ports
    Router#show trunk

DISL = Dynamic Inter-Link Switch

NOTE:

Fast Ethernet uses the Trunking Protocol ISL and 802.1q
between two switches

- Trunk Links are used to transport VLANs between devices and can be configured to transport all VLANs or just a few

- A VLAN Trunk Protocol allows an administrator to add, delete, or rename (modify) VLANs which are then propagated to all the other switches

To configure a trunk interface
Router(config)#trunk [on | off | desirable | auto | nonnegotiate]

To verify the trunk
Router(config)#show trunk [a | b]

To negotiate with the other connected devices

And

To set trunking on the **on** parameter, the other device must be in the on, desirable, or auto state use

Router(config)#**trunk desirable**

To set trunking for a switch port to negotiate with the other side and set trunking on only if the other side's state is on, or desirable, use

Router(config)#**trunk auto**

- If the state is set to **off** it will set the port trunk to off and it will then negotiate with the other side to convert the link to nontrunking

- The **Nonnegotiate** mode will set the port to permanent trunking mode with no negotiation with the other side

- The **on** mode sets the port to permanent ISL trunk mode and negotiates with the other side to convert the link to trunking

VLAN Catalyst Switch

- The catalyst switch is, by default, set to a no-management domain state. The user must manually enable the switch in order to use it, or the switch must receive an advertisement for a domain over a Trunk Link

Question: When will a switch update its VTP database?

Answer: When a switch receives an advertisement that has a higher revision number, the switch will overwrite the database in NVRAM with the new database being advertised

Switches look for a revision number plus 1

Then they will delete and upgrade their database

- The switch fabric = a VLAN group on a switch, or a group of connected switches.

- A switched fabric is a group of switches that share the same VLAN information

- Switches forward broadcasts to all segments.

- To synchronize the switches, the VLAN configuration information that is received from the other switches, must use the **Client and Server Mode**

- If you want a switch to become a server, first make it a **client** so it receives all the correct VLAN information, **then change it to a server**

- The Server and the Transparent modes save information to NVRAM

- The Server and the Client Modes are synchronized

VLAN Access Links

- Access links are only part of one VLAN and are referred to as the **native** VLAN of the port

- An Access link switch will remove any VLAN information before it is sent to an Access link device outside the network

An Access link device cannot communicate with devices outside their VLAN
unless the packet is routed through a router

versus

The Trunk Link which will carry multiple VLANs

- Access links only carry information about one VLAN

- Access link devices cannot communicate with other devices outside the VLAN unless the packet is routed through a router

VLAN 802.1q

- 802.1q was created to allow Trunk Links between disparate switches.

- 802.1q is an IEEE standard for frame tagging

- IEEE 802.1q permits the insertion of a field into the protocol to identify the VLAN

- 802.1q sends VLAN information over FDDI. It uses a SAID field in the frame header to identify the VLAN

- 802.1q permits different vendor switches to co-exist in the same switching fabric

NOTE:

802.1q works with the Cisco Spanning Tree Protocol
by creating a single interface for each
VLAN permitted on the trunk.

When you are working with switches that do not use the 802.1q, the switch will be treated as a single trunk link between the switches, thus permitting only one instance of the Spanning Tree Protocol for all VLANs on the trunk.

VLAN's Dynamic Trunking Protocol

- DTP uses ISL or 802.1q

- DTP is a point-to-point protocol

NOTE:

To have hosts on any device communicate between
VLANs, you need a router

The router must have an interface for each VLAN, or be
able to support ISL

Wide Area Network Routers

- Routers interconnect multiple networks

- Routers filter frames based on their logical address

- Routers assign a **unique logical address** to each individual network

- Routers can separate broadcast domains *as* does a switch

NOTE:

Brouters operate at the Data-Link layer and at the Network layer

A Brouter is composed of a Bridge and a router

Frame Relay Switches

- Transmits multiple data packets in bursts over digital lines

- Lines may be leased

- A T1 line carries 1.544 Mbps

- Data packets are contained inside frames when transmitted over leased lines

ATM Switches

Asynchronous Transfer Mode

- ATM works at the Data Link Layer and at the Physical Layer

- ATM transmits 53-byte fixed-length cells
  (48 + 5)

- ATM carries voice, data, or video in a point-to-point scheme

ATM is uni or bi-directional

ATM can also work with a point-to-multipoint – a root to leaves – parameter

A root to leaves indicates a unidirectional only

- ATM can connect a LAN to a WAN backbone

ATM uses SVCs and PVCs and the connection services of PAR and SMDS

- The ATM switch creates a virtual circuit which is **dynamically established** on demand. It is turned off after the transmission is completed.

- To create a virtual circuit in an ATM switch, first create a virtual **channel.** It must be preconfigured prior the creation of the circuit so it can communicate its data transfers

- An ATM switch is a connection-oriented switch that will utilize circuit-switching and packet-switching capabilities

- ATM will work with multiplexing schemes

- An ATM switch can work with an ATM endpoint. An endpoint is a CSU/DSU, or a workstation, or a router, or a video coder-decoder (CODEC)

- ATM usage is **sporadic**

LAN Switching

FDDI and Ethernet can transmit simultaneously

Problem

you have more collisions which slows the network

To solve collision problems in a LAN Switching environment

Do a LAN segmentation.

When you break up a collision domain, you can decrease collisions.
Also, when you reduce the number of workstations per segment,
you also decrease the collisions.

- A switch forwards packets based on the MAC address in the frame

- A switch will forward all broadcast traffic *(Propagates it)*

LAN Segmentation

One of the main concerns is how to work and control packet collisions. When two devices transmit their separate signals, they will eventually collide into each other, A random amount of inactivity occurs when that happens, slowing down the network. The devices listen, then try transmitting their packets again.

There are two main types of collision *(traffic)* areas. The collision domain and the Broadcast domain.

In the collision domain a series – a group – of devices are connected to each other in the same physical media. That is, they are using the same wire within a single segment.

Switches and Bridges are used to control excessive ethernet collisions by creating additional collision domains. The greater the number, the fewer the collisions

The Broadcast domain connects a series of groups – more than one – in a network composed of several segments.

The router is used to contain the broadcast Domain within its own area of control

NOTE:

The Data-Link Layer is mainly responsible for the handling of LAN segmentation

- LAN segmentation helps the router reduce collisions and creates more bandwidth. This, in turn, helps reduce the delay time between packets sent and received

- The router reduces the number of users per segment which in urn reduces congestion

- Bridges, switches, and routers are used to separate LAN segments into different collision domains.

- The LAN Broadcast reaches into ALL the devices on the LAN.

- Multicast are transmitted to a few devices on the LAN

- LAN segmentation serves as a methodology of decreasing broadcasts

- LAN segmentation uses up to 70% of its resources for local usage and 30% for the router's usage. This is referred to as the 70/30 rule of usage

NOTE:

Ethernet = CSMA/CD

Token Ring / FDDI = token passing

Repeaters

The Local Area Network does not spread its wings very far. Its capability is limited to a building, a small complex, a campus. It won't reach my girlfriend's house. For that, I need WAN. A hot-rod would be nicer, though.

- So, a repeater can extend the maximum distance of a network segment.

- A repeater regenerates the signal.

- The repeater works in the **Physical Layer** of the OSI model.

- A repeater is used to extend the distance of a network segment by regenerating (amplifying) the signal strength of the data that is being forwarded.

- A repeater is a part of the node count in the parameters of distance, nodes, and cabling.

  The 5-4-3 rules applies to repeaters

- A repeater will **not** filter out a broadcast. The signal will propagate errors from one segment to another, adding to the network's CSMA/CD burden

  The repeater will forward all packets

- A repeater **cannot** be administratively controlled

Hubs

- A Hub is also known as a **concentrator**

- A Hub is used in a **bus topology**.

- An **Active** hub regenerates and retransmits the signal

- A Hub will maintain a single broadcast along with a single domain

- The Hub also works in the **Physical Layer** of the OSI model

- A **passive** hub is used in conjunction with workstations, printers, and servers to create a single segment through 10BaseT cabling.

- An **Active** hub incorporates a repeater to support multiple connections at a longer distance by regenerating the signal as a repeater does.

- An Active hubs can filter packets through the usage of SNMP

- The more sophisticated hubs can utilize separate ports that have exclusive access to their own bandwidth, thus eliminating CSMA/CD

- Hubs are the least expensive solution to creating segments in a network

330

Bridges

A Bridge is a layer 2 device. (The Data-Link layer). It will segment a network into multiple smaller segments to extend the length of a LAN. A Bridge uses **software**.

- Segmenting helps to better manage data traffic

- A Bridge can create multiple paths to the same destination.

- Bridges can filter data frames

- Bridges can connect dissimilar media: ethernet thinnet to UTP, or Token Ring

Source-route Bridging works with Token Ring

Router(config)#source-bridge [local | group] [destination]

802.1s - Transparent Bridges work with Ethernet

- A bridge can run SNA with NetBIOS because they are nonroutable protocols

Bridges CANNOT connect a token ring protocol to a CSMA/CD protocol

A translational Bridge uses software in its attempts to connect dissimilar domains

A gateway is used to connect different protocols

- A Bridge isolates local traffic to one physical segment, but non-local and broadcast traffic are forwarded.

- A Bridge can make one collision domain into two smaller collision domains, thereby decreasing the collision domain's size. Obviously!

- Even though a Bridge can create separate collision domains, a bridge will still maintain a single broadcast domain. One B to carry many C's.

- A Bridge reduces traffic that has to cross the logical LAN as well as the Physical segment by using a **Forwarding Table**. A Forwarding Table maintains an entry for every host that identifies the next physical segment.

- Bridges learn the MAC address of each frame packet because Bridges work at the MAC layer of the OSI model. A Bridge is capable of forwarding data frames to other segments and can filter the data frames.

- A Bridge can also be used for *nonroutable* protocols, such as *NetBEUI, SNA, and LAT*

A Bridge makes forwarding decisions with a MAC address
whereas
a Router will use the IP address

- A Forwarding Table learns the address by looking at the source MAC address in the ethernet frame, after which the Bridge will cache the entry in its Forwarding Table.

The Bridge also uses the MAC destination address
to determine where to forward its packets

Advantages of using a Bridge

- A Bridge is manageable, reliable, and scalable

- Problems with using a Bridge

- A Bridge can create loops, and redundancy, delays, and will transmit broadcast storms and multicast storms.

- A Bridge does not provide security.

  Recall this: RIP does not provide security

- A Bridge does not logically separate a LAN. A router does.

Solution

- Use the Spanning Tree Protocol (802.1d) to eliminate loops and broadcast storms.
- as well as IEEE 802.1q

- A Bridge uses Store and Forward in its buffer area

- Bridges do not use routing protocols. A router does.

The Spanning Tree Protocol

IEEE 802.1d

- Use the Spanning Tree Protocol to eliminate loops and broadcast storms.

- The STP is enabled by default

- The STP works by **blocking, listening, learning, and forwarding**

- A Spanning Tree Protocol creates a **root bridge path**.

STP uses Bridge Priority, and Bridge ID (through a MAC address) to determine the Root Bridge election for each VLAN on each switch. There are a maximum of 8 address per network

This is referred to as the port identifier, a layer 2 function: the Data-Link

- After the root bridge path is created, the **path costs** are determined by the other bridges, then every other bridge selects one of its ports that uses the **least path cost**

- Next, the designated bridges are determined by the **lowest aggregate root path cost**

The designated bridge is the only bridge on a LAN that is allowed to forward frames

A Spanning Tree Algorithm sends out BPDUs (Bridged Protocol Data Units)

BPDU's travel in one direction from the root's switch.

Afterwards, the switch will send a configuration BPDU to complete the communication

The Spanning Tree Protocol is applied whenever a Bridge is powered up or, a topology change occurs.

Timers	
The Hello Timer	How often to broadcast
Maximum Age Timer	Determines the amount of time the information is received on a port. This information must expire before the STP can determine that the topology has changed
Forward Delay Timer	Determines the length of time of the listening and learning states before the port begins forwarding

To enable the Spanning Tree Protocol on a specific VLAN
    Router#config t
    Router(config)#spanning-tree vlan [number of vlan]
    Router(config)#exit
    Router#

(The exit returns you to the prompt)

To verify the configuration
    Router#sh spanning-tree vlan [number of vlan]

To configure any of the three timers on a VLAN route
    Router#config t
    Router(config)#spanning-tree vlan [# of vlan]
{forward-time | max-age | hello-time} [# of seconds]
    Router(config)#exit
    Router#

To disable the Spanning Tree Protocol on a specific VLAN
    Router(config)#no spanning-tree vlan [# of vlan]

Switches

A switch is a layer 2 device and works at the Data-Link layer. Its main purpose is to control congestion that is caused through CSMA/CD over shared media. Therefore, it can be stated, that a switch eliminates CSMA/CD because the switch can guarantee bandwidth per port. A Switch makes forwarding decisions based on a MAC address.

- A switch can dynamically learn the MAC address and store it in a table and will create a virtual path to forward the frames to the port where it knows the destination device exists.

- A switch creates a temporary path between the source and destination address

- A Switch creates **multiple broadcast collisions** by creating multiple VLANs.

The path depends on a Router to route the packets between the VLANs

- Switches connect servers and backbones to a LAN and they are capable of utilizing the existing cabling parameters and network adapters

- Switches minimize network traffic to individual network devices

- A switch will create a single broadcast domain and a switch will create separate collision domains. **Hardware** based parameter

- Switches can communicate concurrently and still provide a device with dedicated access

338

- Switches provide faster forwarding rates than routers or bridges

- Switches read the destination address on incoming frames to determine the proper interface to forward the frame out

- Switches help Fast Ethernet with half-duplex and full-duplex

- Switches offer more port densities than Bridges as each port will not fight another port. Each port has their own full bandwidth.

A port density is the number of ports on one physical device

Full-Duplex Switches

A Session Layer Function

3 modes of communication	
Simplex	One device transmits while another listens
Half-duplex	It either transmits or it listens. It uses one pair of wires
Full-duplex	It transmits and receives at the same time. It uses two pairs of wires

- **Switches** provide full-duplex media access

- Full duplex uses a point-to-point connection between two endpoints.

    A switch to a server. A Switch to a Router

- Full duplex transmits and receives at the same time

The fiber-optic cable, under the parameters of 100BaseFX, contains two strands inside the same wrapping

- Full duplex uses virtual circuits: PVC and SVC

Full duplex Ethernet doubles throughput
10 = 20, 100 =200

There are no collisions of frames in full duplex ethernet

To implement Full Duplex Ethernet
All network cards must support full duplex Ethernet, as well as all other connectivity devices
Disable loopback and collision detection methods

Half-duplex Switches

A Session Layer Function

- Half-duplex switches provide a one-way transmit

- Half-duplex transmissions have more frequent collisions

CSMA/CD topology

- A half-duplex switch uses the MAC Layer of the Data-Link Layer whenever it works with Gigabit Ethernet

- The default option is set for 10Mbps TX ports

To configure the full duplex or half duplex switches on a router
    Router#config t
    Router(config)#ip address 123.45.67.8 255.255.255.0
    Router(config)#int e1
    Router(config-if)#duplex [auto | full | full-flow-control | half]
    Router(config-if)#^Z
    Router#

Of course, to verify the duplex settings on the interface, type
    Router#sh int

SIMPLEX

A Simplex switch can only transmit when the line is clear. It must wait for the message to be received before it can accept a reply.

Similar to the Old Ham Radios

Cut-through Switching

- Cut-through Switching reads only the destination address of a packet before forwarding the entire frame

- Cut-through Switching conducts a search in its **switch table** for the destination port

- Cut-through Switching, however, provides **no error checking**

- Cut-through Switching has the **lowest latency**

- Thus, cut-through Switching increases throughput

- Cut-through Switching makes decisions at **wire-speed**

- Cut-through Switching works with **multi-media** applications that require minimal delays in data transferring

---

Cut-through switching uses the first 6 hexadecimal bytes of a MAC address
to immediately begin forwarding the packets

versus

Fragment Free which only reads the first 64 bytes of a frame before forwarding it to its destination

---

NOTE:

A Switch can use both: cut-through and fragment-free switching

Fragment-Free Switching

- The fragment-free switching mode is incorporated as a backbone application in a congested network.

- It only examines the first 64 bytes of a packet

IEEE 802.3 regulates runts and giants

Problem

You are limited to a 10Mbps network

NOTE:

A case is made for using the **Error-Free Switching** because it can quickly read the MAC address and the CRC for each frame.

If the CRC is correct, it will forward the frame to its destination.

If incorrect, off it goes to the Store and Forward switching environment

Store-and-forward Switching

- Store-and-Forward switching copies a packet to its **buffer** area

- It **performs error checking** on the packet frame before it is sent to its destination

- Store and Forward has **higher latency** than cut-through switching

   However, greater frame throughput is performed by cut-through switching

   Store-and-forward switches read the entire incoming frame
   and copies the frame into its frame header before forwarding

- Store-and-forward switching perform CRC (cyclical redundancy check)

- If an error occurs, a store-and-forward switch will drop the frame

- If no errors, store-and-forward will check its forwarding table to determine the proper path

   Ports = unicast and multicast

- The Store and Forward will discard frames that contains errors

CRC is performed inside Store and Forward's buffers

- Store and Forward Switches will discard **runts**, a frame that has less than 64 bytes

- Store and Forward Switches will discard **giants**, a frame that has more than 1518 bytes

NOTE:

A Bridge, a Switch, and a Router
use Store and Forward

Switch versus Bridge

Both are Layer 2 devices - Data-Link

Switch

- A Switch provides increased port density and more forwarding capabilities.

- A Switch allows LANs to be microsegmented

- A Switch **increases** the bandwidth delivered to each device

- A Switch learns addresses, makes forwarding and filtering decisions, and avoids loops

Bridge

- A Bridge is a device that is used to physically segment a LAN into multiple physical segments.

- A Bridge uses a Forwarding Table to determine which frame needs to be forwarded to specific segments.

- If the destination address is unknown to the Bridge, it will forward the packet to all ports except the originating port

- A Bridge does **isolate local traffic** and it does filter the originating physical segment, however, it will also **forward all non-local and broadcast traffic**

- Should it happen that a packet has a source and destination address on the same segment, the packet will be discarded by the Bridges using that segment

Both bridges and switches can read the MAC address

NOTE:
Both create separate collision domains, yet, both still maintain a single broadcast domain

Don't forget about the cable hookup formula

Straight through = unlike devices, and it uses the color codes on its end connectors

Crossover = alike devices

Routers

- A Router is a layer 3 (Network Layer) device that uses the IP address to forward packets. To accomplish this, the router must discard the Data-Link header and trailer.

The trailer holds the FCS / CRC for error-checking

- A Router joins multiple networks together

- A Router filters frames based on logical address

- A Router assigns logical addresses and unique numbers

- A Router isolates one logical LAN from another logical LAN

- A Router isolates traffic into logical and physical LANs

- A Router creates separate domains and separate collision domains

(Bridges and Switches physically segments LANs)

- Routers can interconnect different LAN topologies, different LAN media, and different media access methods

The key to connecting a Token Ring to an ethernet, or a CSMA/CD
to a token bus is for the router to share a common protocol:
IPX to IPX or IP to IP

Yes, a Gateway can connect an IPX protocol to an IP protocol

- Routers are easier to manage
- They are better at flow control
- They can create **multiple active** paths
- They incorporate **explicit packet lifetime** control methods

NOTE:
On a flat network, to stop a broadcast domain, you need to use a router.

A router will keep the broadcast storm within the originating network.

Router Summary

- Routers reside at the Network Layer of OSI Model = path determination

- Routers are used to segment a network

- Routers do not pass broadcast traffic

- Routers filter by IP address and create a routing table

Routers DO NOT filter by MAC addresses because
A MAC address is a Data-Link Layer function – layer 2

A router uses the IP address to make a packet forwarding
decision
whereas
a Bridge will use the MAC address

- A router can act as a firewall

A router can act as a gateway link between a corporate network and the Internet

Use access-lists to enforce security

- You can administer the router from a remote location through the usage of **SNMP**

- A router uses Store and Forward

- A Router uses Routing Protocols. They discard the Data-Link header and the trailer.

- A Router uses the TCP/IP Application Layers: Telnet, TFTP, DNS, and SNMP

Switch versus Router

Switch

- Collisions will be deceased

- Some traffic can stay localized

- Network throughput can be increased

- Increased latency

- A switch forwards packets based on the MAC address in the frame

Router

- Network security can be more easily controlled

- Broadcast traffic is minimized

- The network is more scalable, with greater functionality

- Network traffic can be managed and controlled more efficiently

- A router is harder to configure than a switch on a network

- You can establish multiple paths with lower throughput, even though your overhead will increase

- Whenever you use acknowledgement-oriented protocols, your router will experience a 30-40% decrease in its throughput

Gateways

- Translates communication protocols between dissimilar LAN's

- Can connect a PC to a mainframe

- A Gateway can connect an IPX protocol to an IP protocol

LAN Protocol Technologies

FDDI = ANSI X3T9.5

Ethernet = 802.3

Token-Ring = 802.5

ARCnet = ANSI 878.1

ARCnet is a token passing topology that uses RG-62 cable

Attached Resources Computer Network

Netflow Switching

Caches destination IP address, the source netflow address, and the upper-layer TCP or UDP ports.

A 2600 series router, after version 12.0, uses netflow switching

- With netflow switching the router will cache the entire 32-bit destination if there are multiple equal cost, nondefault paths.

- If the router uses the default route to send a packet, it only caches the major network number and not the entire 32-bit address

- The router load shares on a per-packet basis **(round-robin)**

- The router will not place multiple interfaces in the fast switching cache for the same destination.

Switches	
Autonomous Switches	Packet compression
Fast Switching	used when no online exists in the cable
Optimum Switching	used in high-end routers
Process Switching	packet goes to the buffer, address is looked up, encapsulated, then forwarded

Access lists

An access list is applied to an interface.

An interface represents an I/O port that is built into a router and referenced by its number:

Serial 0, serial 1, ethernet 0, ethernet 1

A group of ports on a common adapter card is represented by:
Interface serial slot # / port #

- An access list is an ordered set of commands that **permits** or **denies** the flow of packets across an interface based on a **match criteria** of access list parameters and the information contained in the packets.

- Access lists must be created   **then**   applied to an interface

- Dynamic access lists are also known as "lock-and-key security"

- Dynamic access lists permits the coding of IOS statements

- The statements in the configuration file are stored in ASCII. They are displayed on the router's console terminal or on a remote terminal

- When using a text editor, save the new file as an ASCII text (.txt) file. The new file is now stored in NVRAM and loaded into the upper-addressed memory area

- Implicit masks are implied but not stated. The **deny all** implicit mask is at the end of every access list

A wildcard-mask works in reverse of a subnet mask.

A binary 1 represents no match while a binary 0 represents a match

- The keyword "host" signifies an **exact match** and represents the wildcard-match of **0.0.0.0.**

(To specify ALL hosts, the wildcard use of 191.39.0.0 = 0.0.255.255)

- The world **only** is also used to signify one specific ip address or protocol usage or network or node / device.

- **Any** is used as an abbreviation for a source address and a wildcard-mask of 0.0.0.0 255.255.255.255

Router(config)#access-list 29 permit any
is the same as
Router(config)#access-list 29 permit 0.0.0.0 255.255.255.255

*This statement **specifies** that an IP access list command can either permit or deny traffic from **any** IP address*

To clear all PREVIOUS matches from an access list
    clear access-list counters [#]

To see the list of different types of access lists
    Router#config t
    Router(config)#access-list ?

The ? follows a space

This will display the list of different types of access lists on your router

To **verify** all the access lists in **use and configured** on a
router
And
To view a specific access list designation
Router#show access-lists
Or
Router#show ip access-lists   *(Hyphens are*
required)

To monitor the Access Lists
Router#sh access-lists

After you typed and viewed the above command, type
Router#sh run

Router#show access-lists

- Displays all the configured access-lists on the router

- Displays all the protocols

- Displays all the interfaces

- Displays the contents of the access lists

Do not confuse this command with
Router#show interface

Subnet Matching of the Range Parameters

To create an access list that presents all users on
subnetwork 12.12.128.0
using the subnet mask 255.255.192.0 from being able to
telnet anywhere, do this

Router(config)#access-list 155 deny tcp 12.12.128.0
0.0.63.255 any eq telnet

To discover the **range** of the submask, do this:

wildcard	255.255.255.255
subtract the subnet mask	- 255.255.192.255
= subnet range	0. 0. 63.255

Disregard the subnetwork statement 12.12.128.0
as the discovery process is only concerned with the subnet
mask range

Question: What wildcard mask can we use to **include** the range of Ip address between 189.234.156.192 through 189.234.92.112?

To discover the wildcard mask range within a specified IP group of IP addresses, do this:

	The greater number of IP address	189.234.156.192
subtract	The lowest number of IP address	- 189.234. 92.112
	= wildcard	0. 0. 64. 80

The range must be using same Class of addresses, where the network octets match

The Anwser is:
   Router(config)#access-list 29 permit 189.234.156.192 0.0.64.80

Q: What is the first command to create an access list that will prevent all users on subnetwork 189.234.156.0 from using the subnet 255.255.224.0 from getting e-mail?

A: Router(config)#access-list 123 deny tcp 189.234.156.0 0.0.31.255 any eq smtp log

Subtract 255.255.255.255 from 255.255.224.0 = 31.255

I placed the log argument in the statement so you can visualize its usage

Access lists Common Ranges

1-99	ip standard
100-199	ip extended
800-899	ipx standard
900-999	ipx extended
1000-1099	IPX SAP
300-399	DECnet
600-699	AppleTalk
700-799	48 bit MAC address

To see which interfaces have access groups set on them
   Router#show ip interface

To **view** the IP access list that has been **applied** to a
specific interface
and
To view the ports which have an IP address list applied to
them
   Router#show ip interface
Or
   Router#show running-config

Access lists Extended IP

These protocols are used in the protocol argument of the CLI	
ip	Internet Protocol
ipinip	IP in IP tunneling
ospf	OSPF routing protocol
tcp	Transmission Control Protocol
udp	User Datagram Protocol
gre	Cisco's GRE tunneling
esp	Encapsulation Security Payload
icmp	Internet Control Message Protocol
igrp	Internet Gateway Message Protocol
eigrp	Cisco's EIGRP routing protocol
ahp	Authentication Header Protocol
nos	KA9Q NOS compatible IP over IP tunneling

Integer in the range of 0-255

The Extended range is from 100-199

Access-list [100-199] [Permit | Deny] [Protocol | Protocol argument]
[Source source-wildcard | **any**] [Destination destination-wildcard]
[operator   precedence precedence #] [port tos tos]
[log]

*The **any** statement goes in the source parameter*

An extended IP access list can filter or deny traffic by using:

- Source Address
- Destination IP address
- The protocol
- The port number

To connect and to link together an access list 111 inbound to interface e1
    Router(config-if)#ip access-group 111 in

NOTE:

Place the extended access list as **close** to the **source** as possible

TCP port number = 6

UDP port number = 17

1) It is best to **deny first,**

2) then type in the **source address** that you want to filter,

3) then type in a **permit** statement.

For Example:

Router(config)#access-list 123 deny tcp host
123.45.67.1 host 123.45.68.1 eq telnet
Router(config)#access-list 123 permit udp any host
144.123.12.1 eq smtp
Router(config)#^+Z
Router#

To **apply** use the **access group** command
Router#config t
Router(config)#int e0
Router(config-if)#ip access-group 1 out
Router(config-if)^ + Z
Router#

Don't forget: the Router#show access-lists and the Router#show ip access-lists are used to verify the applied command

You need to use hyphens in the terms access-list and access-group

To allow **only** www traffic into network [ip address]
    Router(config)#access-list 111 permit tcp any [ip address] 0.0.0.255 eq www

Access lists Standard IP

The Standard range is 1-99

A source IP address as well as a range of source IP addresses
can be used to deny traffic

Access-list [access-list number 1-99] [permit | deny] [IP address] [wildcard mask] [log]

The wildcard mask and log arguments are optional

255 = matches any number in the range that appears in the fourth octet
0 = must match exactly the number in the fourth octet range

The word **host or only** can be used to represent the numbers 0.0.0.0

When you use host you are asking the access list to check for a specific address

The word **any** refers to:
255.255.255.0
255.255.0.0
255.0

It states to the access list that you are not concerned about the IP address

A filter separates data, signals, or material

To remove an access list
    Router#config t
    Router(config)#no access-list 67
    Router(config)#int e0
    Router(config-if)#no ip access-list 67 out
    Router(config-if)#^ + Z

To allow **only** traffic from network [ip address] to enter interface serial1
    Router(config)#access-list 9 permit [ip address] 0.0.255.255
    Router(config)#int s1
    Router(config-if)#ip access-group 9 in

in = enter

To create an access list
    Router#access-list 67

To apply the access list to an interface
    Router#config t
    Router(config)int e1
    Router(config-if)#ip access-group 67 out
    Router(config-if)#^ + Z
    Router#

To verify the access list in your router
    Router#sh access-list

To see a list of all **IP** access lists that exists in the router
    Router#sh **ip** access list   *(There is no hyphen in the IP command)*

To see which access lists are applied to an interface
    Router#show ip int e0
Or
    Router#show ipx int e0

To see a list of all the IP access lists that are currently in use in interface s0
    Router#show ip interface s0

To see in s1
    Router#sh ip interface s1

To see in e0
    Router#sh ip int e0

To see in e1
    Router#sh ip int e1

To permit **only** traffic to or from network [ip address] to be allowed through a specific Class A interface
    Router(config)#access-list 1 permit [ip address] 0.0.0.255

NOTE

Place **standard** access lists as close to the **destination** as possible

Place **extended** access lists as close to the **source** as possible

or

standard = destination

extended = source

To see what lines in IP access list 80 were matched by the traffic that passed through the router
    Router#show ip access-list 80

To permit **only** one host from network 123.45.67.1 to enter a network
    Router(config)#access-list 67 permit 123.45.67.1 0.0.0.0

To allow traffic from **all** hosts on network 123.45.0.0
    Router(config)#access-list permit 123.45.0.0 0.0.255.255

0.0.255.255 is a wildmask

To deny traffic from host 123.45.67.8

    Router(config)#access-list 89 deny 123.45.67.8 0.0.0.0

Named lists

After Cisco IOS 11.2 you can use named lists

Named lists do not have a limitation of 99 entries in the Standard or 100 in the extended and the name lists can be edited.

Access lists Extended IPX

An Extended IPX range is from 900-999

To create an extended access list
    Router(config)#ipx access-list [access-list number 900-999] [permit | deny] protocol [source-network] [destination] [destination-node-mask]

(node-mask is the same as socket)

A socket is composed from the ip address, the node, and the protocol

To apply an extended access list
    Router(config-if)#ipx access-list [access-list-number 900-999] [in | out]

> -1 signifies **ALL** networks **in both**
> the source
> and destination networks

If you want to filter IPX traffic by IPX socket number, use an extended IPX access list

To see a list of all the IPX access lists that are currently in use on the router

Router#show ipx access lists

There is no hyphen in the IPX command line

To permit traffic to pass between network 8 and network 18 and apply the new configuration

access-list 999 permit -1 8 18

ipx access-group 999

In this situation the **-1** *lets you know that you are using a protocol*

Also, a -1 means all networks

Access lists Standard IPX

A Standard IPX range is from 800-899

To create a standard IPX access-list
Router(config)#access-list [access-list-number 800-899] [deny | permit] source-network

Don't forget: IP standard uses only the source network

Here is a more complete access-list command that provides various options to be added:
[.source-node] [source-node-mask] [destination-network] [.destination-node] [destination-node-mask]

To apply access list 899 to the outgoing serial interface of the router
Router(config-if)#ipx access-group [access-list number] [out | in]
Or
Router(config-if)#ipx access-group 899 out

To deny IPX network 33 access to IPX network 3
Router(config)#access-list 812 deny 33 3

To deny IPX network 30 access to IPX network 4
Router(config)#access-list 800 deny 30 4

When you have a single corporate network office, numbered 66, and it connects to three IPX networks numbered 123, 124 and 200 and you desire to allow traffic to access networks 123 and 124 but block access to network 200, do this:

```
access-list 888 deny 66 200
access-list permit -1 -1
```

Access lists IPX SAP

Range 1000-1099

Access-list [list number 1000-1099] [permit | deny] source service type

To control the amount of SAP advertisement traffic that is passed by the router
    Router(config)#access-list 1111 deny -1 11
Or
    Router(config)#access-list 1111 permit -1

To apply this access-list to the **outgoing** serial interface 0 of the router
    ipx output-sap-filter 1111

To see the interface to which ipx SAP access list 1111 has been applied
    Router#show ipx interface

There is no hyphen in the IPX command line

To apply to the **incoming** traffic
and
To **stop** SAP table update entries
    Router(config)#ipx input-sap-filter 1000

To block a router from advertising SAP file servers for a specific server

And

to **stop** SAP default updates *(every 60 seconds)*
    Router(config)#access-lists 1001 deny 1099
    Router(config)#ipx output-sap-filter 7

SAP Filters	
Printer	7
router	98
File server	4

To see if your router is receiving SAP and RIP information on an interface

    Router#show ipx int

To see if the router is receiving the SAP broadcast
Or
To verify that a router is advertising SAP services, their network addresses
and their NetWare servers

    Router#show ipx servers

Access lists Other Arguments

IPX NetBIOS access lists

These restrict IPX network Basic Input/Output system (NetBIOS) traffic based on NetBIOS names

Reflective Access Control list

Maintains pseudostate information
Not good for FTP usage

- Used to create dynamic openings in an access list on an as-needed basis for supporting single-channel applications

- Cisco routers use Access Lists to identify packets for encryption

- Only one access list is allowed per interface

Context-Based Access Control Lists

- CBAC supports multichannel applications

- Java blocking can be performed with CBAC

- CBAC provides a real-time alert and audit trail.

TCP Intercept

- Syn Flooding is used to prevent hacker attacks

- CHAP authentication methods can overload a Web server

Data Circuit-Terminating Equipment

- DCE is used to connect a DTE to a line or to a network

  (use a DCE modem that uses a clocking signal)

- DCE devices between the LAN and the DTE perform data translation between the LAN and the DTE

To see information about the physical interface
Router#sh controllers s0

(This shows the DTE cable or the DCE cable)

(CSU/DSU is used to communicate over digital lines)

- DCE devices are modems, CSU/DSUs, Frame Relay Switches, and TA/NT1s

  (DCE modems communicate over analog lines)

To add bandwidth of a serial link as well as the clock rate
Router(config-if)#bandwidth 56

(Bandwidth is in kilobits.)

*There is no space in the word bandwidth
as it is a single word*

To add a clock rate of 56 kbps
Router(config-if)#clock rate 56000

Clock Rate is in bits.
In most routers there is a dividing space between clock and
rate
as they are treated as two separate words. However, this is
not always the case.

NOTE:

Clock rate and bandwidth are rendered (config-if)#

Data Communication Equipment

- A DCE attaches to the DTE and to a router

- The DCE provides the clocking signal

- The DCE converts data into a switched format

- The DCE switches the data across the providers network

- A DCE can use a CSU/DSU

To find out if a specific interface was configured as DCE or DTE
    Router#show controller serial
Or
    Router#show controllers
Or
    Router#show controller serial1

NOTE:

The console port on a router is designated as the DCE

In a back-to-back setup using DTE/DCE cables,
*hook the cable to the **serial port** on the DCE router*

The CSU/DSU can be used as a digital interface device that
adjusts
the physical interface in a DTE to the interface of a DCE.

The CSU/DSU provides the signaling timing for
communication
between the DTE and DCE.

The DCE provides the clocking mechanism.

Data Terminal Equipment

- DTE is the default router device that acts as a gateway to the local network

- A DTE receives the clocking signal from the DCE

- DTEs are used in virtual circuits

- A virtual circuit must connect two DTE devices within a Frame Relay network

- A DTE is considered a Non-ISDN terminal that predates the ISDN standards. The DTE can be used as a TE2 device

- The DTE end of a proprietary Cisco 60 pin connector is used to connect from the back of your router's serial port to a T1 line. The service provider will provide the connector on the DCE end of the cable.

There are two kinds of cables: straight through and crossover.

Straight through cable is used to hook up unlike devices:

A Switch to a router or a server or a PC
A Hub to a server or a PC
whereas
A Crossover cable hooks up alike devices

A Switch to a switch, a hub to a hub

The DTE uses an **Access link**, which is a leased line, to reach the DCE

NOTE:

The CPE, Demarc, DCE and the DTE are used within the WAN parameters

Don't forget about the LAPB usage under the guidelines of ABM in the HDLC

DTE Devices

multiplexers, protocol translators, computers

A DTE device can also be the router that acts as the gateway to the local area network

A DCE is the device between the LAN and the DTE that performs
the data translation between the LAN and the DTE

- In an X-25 session a DTE device communicates with another DTE device

- A DTE can communicate across a X-25 network. The DTE is used to establish or terminate a X.25 session

(X.25 uses a PAD (Packet assembler/disassembler)
between the DTE and DCE
to buffer and to reassemble or disassemble packets)

- To simulate a WAN connection using a DTE/DCE cable you must activate the clock rate command to a router interface that is connected to another router with a DTE/DCE cable

The clock rate command instructs the router interface to provide the clocking
on the line normally provided by the CSU/DSU device

To set the clock rate
Router(config-if)#clock rate 56000

NOTE:

The Auxiliary port on a router is DTE. (EIA/TIA.232)

The DTE uses a modem for asynchronous communication

It is the DLCI that is used to identify a logical connection
between DTE devices

Customer Premise Equipment

- The CPE resides at a customer's site, where the devices connect to a terminal, to the PC, to the router, and to a modem

CPE can be considered as terminating equipment that is owned by the customer

- The telephone company, however, owns the demarc. Yet, **the demarc** that contains all the customer's equipment that is necessary to go to the Central Office **is located** at the customer's site.

- CPE uses SIP (Subscriber Network Interface) to communicate between the CPE and the SMDS network equipment

The CPE needs to convert a SNI from the router to the SMDS WAN through the ISP's equipment

The SNI works through SIP as a connectionless service

Modems

- Transmits digital data in an analog form using plain old telephone service (POTS)

- Modems use existing telephone lines

CSU/DSU

- A channel service unit/data service unit is a device required by a router to transmit and receive data from a Frame Relay network link.

- The device reformats a router's digital signals to and from a leased line's digital signal

NOTE:
The SMDS is a WAN Protocol that utilizes
packet-switching technology
over the public data networks (PDN)
at speeds of 1.544Mbps

LOCAL LOOP & DEMARC

Cabling that extends from the demarc to the telephone company's Central Office (CO)

DEMARC

- The Demarcation point begins at the customer's site.

- This is where the devices connect. After they connect, the cabling proceeds to the Central Office.

NOTE:

The customer owns the DTE (the Routers),
the CPE (the computers, the printers, the scanners),
the DCE,
Yes, he can even own the Local Area Network (all the stuff inside the building,
the building itself, the territory surrounding it,
and in a manner of speaking, he even owns the employees.

However, the customer does not own the Central Office nor the Demarc, nor the T1 line.

Quick Facts

- Hop counts are dynamic

- Metric counts are static

- MTBF is Mean Time Between Failure

  MTBF is used to measure availability

- Triggered updates speed up convergence by immediately notifying the neighbor routers

- AppleTalk network address are divided into three phases

1 Network Number   16 bits
2 Node Number   8 bits
3 Socket Number   8 bits

- Multiplexing allows multiple data paths to be combined into one channel. Several logical signals can be converted into one physical signal for transmission across a single physical channel. Uses Ports!

AppleTalk Phase II address format				
network	.	node	.	socket
55	.	6	.	1

AppleTalk uses RTMP to create Routing Tables

(Routing Table Maintenance Protocol = Distance Vector)

Author's Autobiography

Walter Schenck has studied and worked on computers for a number of years. In addition to his CCNA, A+, ENP, MCP, MCSE and AutoCAD he holds numerous other certifications in the computer field.

NOTES

www.ingramcontent.com/pod-product-compliance
Lightning Source LLC
Chambersburg PA
CBHW051044050326
40690CB00006B/592